75
FSG

JAN GRUE

I Live a Life Like Yours

Translated from the Norwegian by B. L. Crook

Jan Grue is the author of a wide-ranging body of work in fiction, nonfiction, children's books, and academic literature, and a professor at the University of Oslo. *I Live a Life Like Yours* was published in 2018 in Norway, where it won the Norwegian Critics Prize for Literature and was nominated for the Nordic Council Literature Prize; it was the first Norwegian nonfiction book to be so honored in fifty years.

B. L. Crook is a writer and literary translator. In 2010, she founded *SAND*, an English-language literary journal, in Berlin. She led creative writing workshops in the Netherlands for two years before returning to the United States. She lives with her family on an island near Seattle.

I Live a Life Like Yours

I Live a Life Like Yours

a memoir

Translated from the Norwegian by B. L. Crook

Jan Grue

FSG ORIGINALS
FARRAR, STRAUS AND GIROUX
NEW YORK

FSG Originals
Farrar, Straus and Giroux
120 Broadway, New York 10271

Originally published in Norwegian in 2018 by Gyldendal Norsk Forlag AS, Norway, as
Jeg lever et liv som ligner deres
English translation published in the United States by Farrar, Straus and Giroux
First American edition, 2021

Grateful acknowledgment is made for permission to reprint "The Man in the Iron Lung" by Mark O'Brien. Copyright © 1999, Lemonade Factory—a small press. Used by permission.

Library of Congress Cataloging-in-Publication Data
Names: Grue, Jan, 1981– author.
Title: I live a life like yours : a memoir / Jan Grue ; translated from the Norwegian by
    B.L. Crook.
Other titles: Jeg lever et liv som ligner deres. English
Description: First American edition. | New York : FSG Originals / Farrar, Straus and
    Giroux, 2021. | Summary: "In this essayistic autobiography, Jan Grue reflects on
    social structures, disability, loss, relationships, and the body: in short, on what it
    means to be human" —Provided by publisher.
Identifiers: LCCN 2021011635 | ISBN 9780374600785 (paperback)
Subjects: LCSH: Grue, Jan, 1981– | College teachers—Norway—Biography. |
    People with disabilities—Norway—Biography.
Classification: LCC LA2375.N62 G7813 2021 | DDC 378.1/25092 [B]—dc23
LC record available at https://lccn.loc.gov/2021011635

Designed by Janet Evans-Scanlon

Our books may be purchased in bulk for promotional, educational, or business use.
Please contact your local bookseller or the Macmillan Corporate and Premium
Sales Department at 1-800-221-7945, extension 5442, or by email at
MacmillanSpecialMarkets@macmillan.com.

www.fsgoriginals.com • www.fsgbooks.com
Follow us on Twitter, Facebook, and Instagram at @fsgoriginals

10 9 8 7 6 5 4 3 2 1

This translation has been published with the financial support of NORLA.

For my parents and sister.

For Ida.

I Live
a Life
Like
Yours

From time to time I cross paths with someone who knew me as a child but never expected to meet me as an adult. Out of common courtesy, they are usually able to conceal their surprise at seeing me out in the world until an opening, a gap in the conversation, allows them the space to articulate their initial reaction: *So, you're still alive?*

My junior high ethics teacher once told a story. When her husband died, she cut off her long hair. Afterward, she sank beneath the water in her bathtub. This she experienced as a purification. She was interested in rituals, and she brought a measure of gravity to her class that I valued, as an extremely grave fourteen-year-old. I wanted to learn as much as possible. Time, it seemed, was running out.

My ethics teacher taught me the term *liminal phase*. It describes the most vulnerable part of a rite of passage, the point at which one finds oneself between worlds. It is the period in which a young person is no longer a child, though not yet an adult, or when the dead have abandoned the world of the living but cannot yet be counted as ancestors. During these phases, things can go drastically wrong. But they are also where transformation takes place. We come into being in these phases. Without them, the world could not go on.

I progressed from junior high to high school and then on to university. And then, one day, I ran into my old teacher again, at a conference. She had gone to graduate school, her master's thesis was on Norse mythology, on the Jotuns, symbolic of the dark and treacherous aspects of human existence. I was a doctoral student in linguistics. I had begun an in-depth study of rhetoric, and how reality may be altered through language. She had written a history of mentalities, about modes of thinking that we can no longer fathom. Our worlds had reconvened, in a sense.

My old teacher wasn't surprised to hear that I was pursuing my doctorate. The junior high school was a ten-minute walk from the university library, where I once used my mother's card to borrow books on the shamanism of indigenous Siberian tribes. I was familiar with academia from childhood, and it showed, it shaped others' impressions of me. It promised a particular kind of future, in the same way that the opening sentence of a book points to how the story is going to unfold.

She was, however, surprised at *how good I looked*. This was the other narrative of the future, the one that didn't have to do with my language, but with my body.

This phrase makes me feel uncertain: *You look so good*. Yes, don't I? I dress nicely. I've spent time educating myself about cut, about style. I got a tailored coat when I was eighteen. I like coats with cuffs that can be unbuttoned, and oxford shirts with collars that roll the right way.

But that wasn't what she meant.

What lies beneath—the surprise that I am still alive—surfaces only later in the conversation. Or at least this is what happened with an author I knew from high school. Ten years later we stood together in the grand ballroom of Oslo's Hotel Bristol. With a blend of melancholy and reluctance, her eyes mild, she remarked that it was something they all knew back then, the fact that I was not going to live for very long.

Something they all knew? This wasn't something *I* knew. And since I certainly was not the person who had put this idea in their heads, where did it come from? The author I knew from high school couldn't say. The notion had simply existed. It was a shadow cast by nothing. The only substantial point of reference was my body. In those days, I often rode in a wheelchair, but I had also frequently crossed the schoolyard on foot. I used to go out during breaks and stand around with everyone else in a circle. We would talk about our teachers, we would talk about *Ulysses* too, and joust over who had read the furthest in that book, that's the kind of school it was. I thought I was just

one among many. I didn't know that I was projecting a particularly tragic aura.

I did know. I didn't have the words to express
it. I am trying, now, to find them.

I follow a timeline that others might have followed. I live in the same city where I grew up.
I am an academic, a child of academics. I live
a life like theirs. I am married and have a child
with Ida, who is a woman who writes. My son
has my eyes, which are my mother's eyes, his face
has features reminiscent of childhood photographs of his grandfather. These are the threads
that hold my life together. This is the fabric.

Whenever I am recognized by someone who
recalls the child I once was, a rift occurs, a rup-
ture. The image is jarred. The life I live is dis-
placed, briefly, by a reality that never happened,
it glides past like a specter, depicting opaque but
familiar images, phantom images of an alternate
future that followed me until I became an adult.

The recognition is followed up by the same
compliment—*You look so good*—and it is that

word *so*, two letters at the center of a polite phrase, that carries everything within it, that which could have been, that which never was.

Did you get better?

No, I say, I am more or less in the same shape that I used to be in, the way I was back then. My wheelchair is the same, I sometimes walk, my health is fine.

But you look like you're better!

Memory plays tricks on us, never more so than when it teams up with our expectations. The past is not what happened then, it is what we are speaking about now.

Shouldn't you be dead?

I have surpassed expectations, I've come out on top, allied with nothing other than my own body, which has lived its life, on its own premises. My body does not know which diagnoses it has been given, what kind of prognoses it has received, and this is good.

Never tell me the odds, as Han Solo once said.

This is me as an adult. This is me as a father. This is my son. He has my eyes, but not my diagnosis. He is also, in more than one way, a result of everything that never happened.

Into the unknown; we do not know where we are headed.
We sail in a leaking vessel, aware we are dying animals.
We dream of Byzantium, bailing with all our strength, we sail together.
We are argonauts, cosmonauts, adventurers, explorers. We are on a journey.

Toward the end of high school and at the start of my twenties, I lived through films.

I went to the cinema on Dronningens gate, summers as well as winters. Once a month, on a Sunday evening, the movie was a surprise—no one knew what was going to be screened until the lights were dimmed. I stood waiting in line with friends. Weekday mornings were for press screenings; I sat alone in the half-empty cinema.

I watched my way through history, from the silent film era on. I wanted to know who all the pivotal directors were, what was important.

After a while, I arrived at Wim Wenders. In *Wings of Desire*, Bruno Ganz plays an angel (sporting a worn dark coat and a ponytail) wandering around Berlin. No one can see him, but he observes, he listens. He places an invisible hand on a shoulder, he is present. The screenplay was written by Peter Handke, I didn't know that back then. An old, blind man is named in the credits as *Homer*; I also didn't notice that back then.

What I did notice was this: the angel becomes human. He falls in love, but it is both easier and more complicated than that. He steps out of eternity and into the moment. The Greeks had two words for time: *kronos* denotes the cosmic sense of time while *kairos* signifies the here and now. It is within *kairos* that we live, and it is into *kairos* that the angel falls. He wants to have everything that exists there, that exists *here*, the sounds and smells and tastes. A cup of coffee, a cigarette, complements to his suit and ponytail; angels who are affixed in film are always affixed in time.

The angel asks, and the angel receives. He becomes human. Now he is mortal. And I knew: *This is true.*

Ida and I are in California, this is just before we travel on to Hawaii. We are as far west as it's possible to get in the world, but now we are going to go even farther west. Five hours by plane out into the middle of the Pacific Ocean, to the group of islands that are more remote than any other, where there are skyscrapers and trafficked streets, but where, when the plane approaches at nighttime, all we see are lights and large dark fields that represent dormant volcanoes.

Our time spent together in California is leisurely. I take time to read books about the place where we are and the place where we are going. I tell Ida about what I have been reading. We tell each other about the books we read. We both want to know what the other is thinking, but we also like hearing ourselves doing the telling. Each new book is an exploration, and through the telling we reinforce the feeling of having traveled some distance, of having gained new land.

We are not going to settle here, we know this. We are in San Francisco for a brief month and have digital return tickets in our email in-boxes. Hawaii is an added luxury before our return. Planning this out-of-the-way detour is my initiative, an extravagant gesture in honor of our first long trip together. At the same time, I print out the return tickets and keep them in my bag because I like the feeling of security it provides.

Our journey has safely defined parameters, but when we return home, we have a decision to make. We've been together for half a year and we've reached a turning point of sorts. We have spent more nights together than apart;

increasingly, Ida has left more of her things behind in my apartment. We are in the process
of becoming interwoven. If we don't move in
together after our return, there will be no going
back, only forward, each person for themselves.
We have a choice. There are no imperatives. We
are free to do whatever we want.

I have a literary idiosyncrasy: I don't like over-
explaining. I don't want to expose my references. It's an idiotic attitude, but changing it
now would be painful. It is not something I
wish to give up. I don't want to be easily ap-
proachable; I want to be understood intuitively.
These are two very different things.

Sometimes I go about imagining that I take
an aristocratic approach to life. In Hawaii, Ida
and I walk past the Royal Hawaiian Hotel, in
the middle of Waikiki Beach, with its coral-
pink walls, where Joan Didion used to stay and
where none of the rooms are under five hundred dollars a night. I feel strongly that that is
where we actually should be staying, in the lap

of luxury, on this our first vacation together. Ever since we found each other, practical questions have begun to seem unreasonable—the cost of something, for instance, or whether or not a place is wheelchair accessible.

My first time in Hawaii, I went with friends from my university. We stayed four people in one room, and my strongest memory of the trip is of trying not to fall over in the shower, taking extreme care walking from the shower to the bedroom in a squeaky pair of Crocs. I remember that I traveled with a manual wheelchair that could only be propelled by one's own strength, so that when the others went outside—for a walk, to go for a swim in the ocean—all I could do was wait politely, in the room or in the rundown hotel restaurant. The air that streamed through the building, which was a pavilion with no clear boundary between indoors and out, was mild like an embrace; it was unlike anything I'd experienced before.

The aristocratic element is characterized by not needing to explain oneself. It is to write, as Didion did about California and Hawaii, as if one has always been at home there, as if one knows all there is to know, as if history and the world are self-evidently one's own, a familiar heirloom, an art object that's been in the family for as far back as anyone can recall. Stephen Fry said that Diana Mosley once told him: *Of course, you never knew Hitler, did you?*

Ida and I travel together, we are newly in love and together we fall in love with the places we visit. Many of them are places I have been to before and I want to tell Ida everything I know about my earlier visits so she can know it too, but I also want not to tell her, not to say anything, so that we can discover it together. Abstractions tell us nothing, old references tell us nothing, if we do not recognize their weight in flesh. Word must become body. We must find out who we are in the world and what the world is to us.

This book is about *becoming human*. For a while, this was my working title, for the angel who becomes human—Wim Wenders's and Peter

Handke's angel—who has stood for a long time on my shoulder.

Yet it was a title that I had to give up. It doesn't belong to me, it belongs to the poet Mark O'Brien. He titled his book *How I Became a Human Being*, he earned it in a different way than me. I must give him precedence.

If anyone is my shadow, in the Jungian sense, it is O'Brien. I am weak, he was weaker. I weigh one hundred twenty pounds; he weighed half that. My muscles are small; his were barely visible. My big electric wheelchair grants me a freedom he never had; he was too vulnerable, too fragile.

The angel from *Wings of Desire* becomes human by falling *down* and *in*, he goes from black-and-white to color, and in falling he injures himself, the first color he sees is that of his own red human blood.

It's different for O'Brien, in his book, he becomes human by rising *up* and *out*, even if the movement from the monochromatic to the colorful is present in his story too, the same longing for sensuality, for corporeal presence.

I can't decide. Is mine a story about falling or rising? Or, is it about going inward—about realizing that I always already *was* human? I am uncomfortable with O'Brien's title; I will let him keep it for himself. I understand his demons, but they are not my own.

Still, while he lived, we had several things in common, one of which is an intimate relationship with machines, a different understanding of physical limitations and physical rhythms than most people have.

O'Brien wrote poems. I write prose. I write on a keyboard, and the words flow, they come out quickly. My greatest challenge is that Latinate words flow too freely, too manically, that the words lose their foothold in the body. I need another foreign word, *logorrhea*, to describe this state.

O'Brien was not plagued by logorrhea. His challenges were quite the opposite of mine. If one is unable to use a keyboard, if breathing is so difficult that much of life must be lived in an iron lung, then each phrase must be as valuable as it is costly, then it is necessary to switch to poetry, where the words are few and the meanings condensed, and where a well-turned expression can house a world. This is what I strive for, as we can strive even for what feels the least natural.

Mark O'Brien, "The Man in the Iron Lung"	*I scream* *The body electric,* *This yellow, metal, pulsing cylinder* *Whooshing all day, all night* *In its repetitive dumb mechanical rhythm.* *Rudely, it inserts itself in the map of my body,* *Which my midnight mind,* *Dream-drenched cartographer of terra incognita,* *Draws upon the dark parchment of sleep.* *I scream* *In my body electric;* *A dream snake bites my left leg.* *Indignant, I shake the gods by their abrupt shoulders,* *Demanding to know how such a vile slitherer* *Could enter my serene metal shell.* *The snake is punished with death,*

The specialty of the gods.
Clamp-jawed still in my leg,
It must be removed;
The dream of the snake
Must be removed,
While I am restored
By Consciousness, that cruelest of gods,
In metal hard reluctance
To my limited, awkward, déclassé
Body electric,
As it whispers promises of health,
Whooshes beautiful lies of invulnerability,
Sighs sibilantly, seraphically, relentlessly:
It is me,
It is me.

How I Became a Human Being was published posthumously in 2003, but Mark O'Brien had finished writing it during his lifetime. He died in 1999, on July 4. I think about him often because he lived in Berkeley, and even though six years passed between the time of his death and my first visit to that city, there were still a lot of people around who had known him, it was a place where many who were like him had lived, and had died just as young. It was a place comprised of activists, academics, relatives, friends. Everyone was familiar with vulnerability.

When I was planning my move to Berkeley for a fellowship and it turned out there wasn't accessible housing available to me after all and the time for my move was drawing near, these people were the first to step in and help me. Foremost among them was Sue, my academic sponsor, a professor of English literature who, when I finally met her face-to-face, reminded me of a yogi or a Buddhist monk. She was a widow, her husband had been in Vietnam and had been exposed to Agent Orange there. Sue had a kind of warmth and presence that I encountered multiple times in California. Eventually, I began to think of it as the presence that one strives for when remembering that time is short. For everyone.

Joan Didion wrote that *a place belongs forever to whoever claims it hardest, remembers it most obsessively, wrenches it from itself, shapes it, renders it, loves it so radically that he remakes it in his own image.* I cannot do this for California, it doesn't belong to me in this way. Instead, it's the reverse: *I* belong to California now or, at least, to my own perception of California, the one I have created for myself.

Mark O'Brien weighed only half of what I do, I, who was small and thin, a *slender* child. I measure my movements in meters, he measured his in millimeters. His childhood and youth went: hospital, hospital, other institutions. No friends, no self-determination, nothing, not until he became an adult, practically speaking, and fought his way to a spot at a university.

The differences between us nonetheless push me further away from the meaning behind the title of his book. I never experienced the trauma of institutionalization. I was always already human. O'Brien was sent away from his family early on, for he was among the last children to have polio—born in 1955, died in 1999. He lived alone for so many years.

Until I was ten, we lived—my parents, sister, and I—in a red house in Lyder Sagens gate in Oslo. Every summer we would go to a little cabin, also painted red, on Nøtterøy Island in Vestfold. It wasn't until I was thirteen that I first went to summer camp, along with other children who *had something*. Up until then, I had never spent so much as a single week in an institutional setting.

And yet.

There is a look, a gaze, a form of recognition. There is a sense of loneliness, a feeling of being a body that no one, least of all one's self, wishes to know. And so, we look each other in the eye after all, Mark O'Brien and I, even if we do it begrudgingly, even if we would prefer to avoid each other's gaze.

There is something else: the question of time. The unlived life has no scope, no dimensions. I am haunted by what could have been, by what did not happen. But can I truly claim to have a foothold in the lived life?

I could go at it chronologically, organize events in succession. This seems reasonable, it gives the impression of order and predictable progression, that what happened was what had to happen, but it is a reconstruction, a rationalization, an illusion. The past appears to be strung up on the wall like the Bayeux Tapestry, but, in fact, it is a projected image, a show of light and shadow, originating from my own memory. It exists *now*, in the moment of this writing, such that the things that happened back then also exist *now*, in how I remember them, in how I write them down. I am writing a version of myself that no longer exists.

I also try reconciling the memories of my childhood, happy and sheltered, with the knowledge, which is also present in these memories, that I was different, and that it was dotted with frequent hostile impulses, discomfort, ill-will.

I ask my parents, and they say, "For us, you were always just Jan."

We have had this conversation many times. On this occasion, we are sitting around the living room table in their house, the house in Villaveien where we moved when I was ten and my sister was seven. It is a bright room in a functionalist house with corner windows that let in the light. Visible through the windows is the ramp that was built leading down from the veranda into the garden. In the old house, the red, Swiss-style villa in Lyder Sagens gate, we lived on the second floor. There was a short flight of stairs up to the entry door and a longer stairwell up to our apartment. My parents decided we had to move. In the new house, they had a room and a bathroom built on the first floor for me.

The ramp in Villaveien is made of metal. I remember many things about this ramp, stumbling on it, scraping my knee, learning to guide the wheelchair up and then turn on the uppermost landing. I can recall both walking and riding the wheelchair around in the garden; either way, the important thing was to get beneath the bushes where the last of the ripe raspberries dangled.

For many years, I found it difficult to believe what my parents told me. I trusted they meant what they said, that *I* was just *me* to them, but at the same time I remember the photo of the three of us, leaning over the ramp's railing. It's the year after we moved into the house, and the photo was in the *Aftenposten* newspaper along with an article about rights that have not been met, about battles that must be fought over and over again. The photograph was taken as a protest against what is wrong and unjust. I understood something back then, too, about the storm that was brewing.

Then my own son was born, and the endless delusions about who he might be, and what I expected, collapsed into the actual child like a quantum miracle. Suddenly, I was able to believe my parents, now that I was a father myself, and could see that a child is themself; of course they are.

I look once more at that photo, and I think of Ida, who we have become together, and there is one other thing I notice now, in this facsimile photograph from the 1992 *Aftenposten*: I see a united front. Against what, against the world? There is something present outside the scope of the photo, something at which we are scowling through the lens of the *Aftenposten* photographer, and this *something* has, if not a name, then a language and a presence. Ida and I are familiar with this *something*, both as a couple and as a family, and every day we aim to keep it away from our door, to keep it outside of the house, where we are together as a family. This something is storm and air pollution, it is whispering and accusatory voices. Even if it is not a part of me, I am able to hear and understand it, I can even mimic its mannerisms. Does this mean, then, that it is a part of me after all, if it is so familiar?

In the book *Time Travel: A History*, James Gleick explains that time travel and memory have the same basic problem: entropy. We uncover layer after layer, and though we believe what we are doing is digging down far enough to reach something older, something more authentic, and purer, what we are actually doing is piling on further complications. We can never be children again, and we know just as little about what it means to be a child as we know about life in the fifteenth century.

We cannot *travel* in time. To do so would require both a starting point and a goal that exist outside ourselves, a past that literally is another country. This would be *kronos*, cosmic time. But this is not where we exist. We are encased in the moment, and we carry it with us. We cannot shrug off the eternal *now*, in which the present becomes the past. We live in *kairos*.

It's the same with memory, which is set and lives within us, it is not a mold for a time that was *then*. Each time I relive a memory, I alter it, ever so slightly, for with each reliving, a new pencil stroke is added.

I revise my manuscript once more. The shifts in language are nearly imperceptible, and in this way the manuscript becomes something different, even if I believe it is the same, an authentic reflection of myself.

Ida and I have become a couple, we have gotten married, we have had a child together. I write as my son turns one year old, he is napping outside in his stroller, beneath the veranda overhang while the rain pours down in buckets, Ida is sitting beside me practicing the piano, playing selections from Ingrid Bjørnov's book of classics, children's songs, and film tunes. The storm is outside.

I try to reconstruct who I was before all of this, this person who is already a stranger to me. I am thirty-six. I can remember being eighteen. I am able to reconstruct it, but this is a decisive action, it is an action with a purpose. Ida begins tentatively with "Over the Rainbow," she plays it over and over again. I could never have imagined this future moment when I was eighteen, not only would I have dismissed it as sentimental, I would also have felt very anxious about it, it would have seemed too intimate to me, too overwhelming.

Writing is fixed in a different way than memory. A saying from one of the oldest writing cultures goes: *The faintest ink conquers the strongest memory*. George Orwell believed keeping a diary was among the best habits a human can have. It forces intellectual honesty. One is not only obliged to remember all the instances in which one was mistaken, but also all of the times when one was in the right—though possibly for the wrong reasons. A diary also offers a correction to the truth of a moment, which always shifts according to what is acceptable. In *Nineteen Eighty-Four*, Winston's first decisive act of rebellion is to write down something that has taken place.

I was never good at keeping a diary. And yet, a record of sorts was kept for me. Voices I know—but which are not *me*—exist in written form. They are much easier for me to access than I thought they were several years ago. For this reason, they are also much stronger in their own way; they possess a kind of dusty, totemic power.

I'm talking about a three-foot-long shelf full of papers given to me by my parents. It may be quite by coincidence that I took these papers after Alexander was born. Regardless, the handover was well timed. I will always be my parents' son, but now I am a parent myself, and I have assumed their habits. Once Ida and I knew we were going to have a child together, I put together a pregnancy binder. As the birth date grew closer, I made a birth binder too. I am used to collecting paperwork. To do so is to leave a trail of bread crumbs, to unspool a red thread behind you. It is a refusal to get lost, it is a claim to the truth.

The stack of papers that I took over from my parents is made up of doctors' notes, clinical descriptions, case histories from hospitalizations, copies of letters sent to municipal and state agencies, travel agencies, and living-aids suppliers.

Reading through these records, as trivial and brittle as they are, nevertheless feels like jumping into a pool of icy water. It doesn't lessen the shock to know that the pond is there, to glimpse it out of the corner of your eye before suddenly one day ripping off your clothes and plunging in. The papers follow a different time line than the one I remember following. It is a different life from the one I remember having lived. Perhaps that isn't so strange, considering it was my parents who read and replied to these letters. They weren't addressed to me, they were about me. But the *me* they are about, I hardly recognize this person, and the time line in the records does not match up with the life I now have. The life depicted in these pages is an alternate and much more sorrowful life, perhaps a shorter life, and, in any case, a life containing little joy. It represents the horizon of expectations.

Their subjects aside, all of these papers have something in common, namely, that they are an attempt to hold someone responsible, someone who refuses to be so held. The travel agency that promised to transport a wheelchair but then forgot or broke its promise. The hospital that neglected to follow up, the governing agencies that did not follow their own rules. Institutions and organizations have a long memory, but only if it serves them. Otherwise, they live and justify their rejections in the now.

The papers reflect two full-time roles, performed for many years by my parents from the very first dubious signs when my myopathy began to manifest, until the end of my teens. The paperwork does not stop there, naturally, but by that point I had begun to take over some of the work myself, I had begun to act as my own secretary and case worker, my own post office and central archive.

Among the papers, one reads:

Clinical note, *3-year-old boy, dark blond with brown eyes, attractive*
June 12, 1984 *and well-proportioned, cracile* [*sic*, most likely meant to read *gracile: thin* or *slender*] *with a generally lean physique, relatively poorly developed musculature but good posture.*
[. . .]
His developments in fine motor skills, language, and intellect appear advanced for his age.
He seemed uninterested in lifting his head, turning over, attempting to pull himself around on the floor, etc. and he

never crawled. However, he was able to sit upright with-
out support at the proper age and was just barely able to
walk at the age of 10.5 months, albeit very unsteadily,
constantly falling flat even up to the age of 2.
Has trouble with stairs and uses his left leg to go up each
step, balance still appears poor. He also struggles to climb.

This is not the beginning, but the beginning
was never documented in writing. The beginning must have been a feeling, a premonition,
that something was not as it should have been. *I*
was *me*, but I was also a child who was *constantly
falling flat*, and the worry that followed could
not be reasoned away.

I visit my parents at their home, my childhood
home. We cover the coffee table with binders
and magazine files of written records, we leaf
through brochures, flyers, subscriptions from
the Norwegian association for muscular disease. They tell me, as they have told me before,
how difficult it was to know. The papers still
exist, but for them, the two- and three-year-old
boy is a memory, he no longer exists, and the
memory of him has been written over by

the six-year-old boy, the ten-year-old boy, the thirty-six-year-old man who is writing this.

We are palimpsests. We are manuscripts in which the writing has been erased and rewritten, erased and rewritten again. Everything fades, everything leaves a trace.

My mother visits my office. She has brought the papers in three plastic bags. We leaf through them once again, and then I put them up on the shelf. We speak as though recounting a war.

There was always something, wasn't there?
There was always something.

These papers are glimpsed from the outside, from the viewpoint of the medical system, the physical therapist, the school system, the municipality, the district, the legal system, travel agencies. It is a viewpoint that regards me as freight, a logistical dilemma.

I read the papers again. And although the text is fixed—these are the same words that were there in 1984, the year I was three and received my first diagnosis—I have changed. Jacques Derrida calls attention to this. The reader is transformed; therefore, the text is also transformed.

A sign outside the Homeowners' Association of the development where Ida, Alexander, and I live—a sign that is from the mid-eighties, when the condos were built—emphasizes that residents' cars are not allowed in the back courtyard. An exception is made for the transport of goods and the handicapped. Transport of *goods*, transport of *the handicapped*: this pairing of words is worth some reflection, side by side, decades after they were first posted on the sign.

Time with an infant is pure *kairos*. I am writing after one and a half years as a father. It is a long *now*, the moment stretches out and swallows the horizon.

In the middle of this moment, I get up. It is a morning in the midst of our first autumn together as parents. Ida has not come in from the other bedroom yet, so I know that the night must have been fairly peaceful. We still have nights like that, nights when Alexander eats and sleeps in tandem, when mother and child continue sleeping together until the early-morning hours, even though these nights are becoming less and less frequent. More often now, the day is off with a bang, without warning, and abrupt and full of wild enthusiasm.

This autumn morning, however, I may still wake up alone, in my own time. The bed is high, raised up on blocks, so that when I sit up and swing my feet out over the edge, they don't reach the floor. Nor would it matter if they did. My ankles are twisted, so I'm unable to stand on my bare feet for more than a few minutes at a time; I prefer not to walk barefoot at all.

My sandals wait on the bedroom floor, wide and stable, with insoles molded to the shape of my feet, insoles that wrap snugly around my foot and heel.

With a tiny shove of effort, I stand. The mattress is springy and gives me extra lift. I reach out and grab the windowsill to stabilize myself, find my balance. I walk over and open the door to listen for sounds of Ida and Alexander, to hear whether the morning routine is already under way. But it is quiet, and I walk to the bathroom.

I stand in my sandals as I brush my teeth, I use the toilet and get up again with the help of the handrail that has been screwed tightly into the wall. I unfold the seat in the shower and sit down, remove my sandals with the tongs that hang on the towel bar, and, with the same tongs, pull the shower curtain shut. These are automatic and natural movements, the type of movements that I undertake each day without thinking about it, without documenting them.

A thousand small moments take place and are lost. Not even the brain that guides the body to carry out the movements registers, let alone documents, their happening.

After the shower, I pull on my sandals once again, stand, walk over to the tall, padded bench, and sit down. Throughout my morning routine, I am rarely standing for more than a few minutes at a time, and the bathroom has been set up for this. I now begin the process of getting dressed. I pull on my socks with a sock aid, an ingenious plastic contraption with straps that has been an object of fascination for Alexander since he was four months old. The sight of it used to make him wave his arms with joy, because he wanted to eat it. I pull on my shoes with a shoehorn, which Alexander also enjoys, I pull up their zippers with a stick that has a hook at one end, and I think about Alexander, who has taken note of all of these aids and has wanted to possess them, wanted them to be his. All of the objects in our apartment are different now, characterized by his relationship with them.

The stick with the hook is a simple broomstick handle with the brush part sawed off. There is a store that sells these kinds of special aid instruments, but they are made of plastic, they are not durable. The store is called Simpler Life, but none of its products are as solid as this broomstick that is made of wood with a hook screwed into one end. This stick with the hook has lasted for fifteen years, and may yet last another fifteen. My father made it for me on the bench in his workshop in the basement of my childhood home.

On this late autumn day, I am able to pull on my shoes before Ida comes into the bedroom with Alexander in her arms. This is a fortunate day, a good morning. It takes me thirty minutes to get ready, as always. This is not a span of time that can be abbreviated in any way, but in the best case I am able to divvy it up, distributing the thirty minutes across the span of an hour, with thirty minutes of baby time somewhere in the middle.

I cannot hurry. This is a sobering bit of evidence in my case and a crucial factor, a gigantic boulder in the middle of the road. I cannot hurry to the subway, because my wheelchair can only go the speed that it goes. I cannot run. If I leave five minutes late from my home, I will arrive five minutes late at my destination. I cannot hurry to the bathroom. If I try to walk faster than my normal speed, I trip and fall. Time is inelastic. I require the time that I require.

On this autumn morning, we can put Alexander in his high chair in the kitchen. I can make porridge and feed him, one smeary spoonful at a time, while Ida takes a shower, this is a good morning. While she showers, I can feel how slowly and how quickly time passes, I sense, once more, what it is to be in the moment with an infant.

How long do you need to get ready, Ida, half as much time as I do, a third? You can stand up while showering, you can pull on your clothes while standing, you are able to get ready more quickly if you must, and on most days you must. Time is elastic and never stretches far enough. But I can give you a small bit of time to yourself while I feed Alexander, and when you come out again, I can wipe off his face and bib and high chair while you make us coffee, and the pale sun is on its way up outside the kitchen window.

Each day we continue our journey into the unknown. We find out what we can and cannot do. We explore the unfamiliar land, terra incognita, one day at a time.

At the end of the street where I grew up was the entrance to a park. Stensparken used to be an old execution ground, the kind of location that's straight out of the history books. When my parents moved into the neighborhood at the end of the 1970s and built a family home from the leftovers of an old three-story villa, it was still not uncommon to find used hypodermic needles in the park. Executioners and execution grounds and hypodermic needles. It was a lot of work for them to turn a part of the old house into a new living space, work they did themselves, with grade B planks and skills recalled from high school woodshop classes.

On the opposite side of the park was a tram stop. The tram ran all the way up to a loop in the tracks, and from the loop there was an avenue leading up to the school; it was called an avenue because the trees ran in rows up along either side, like Bygdøy Avenue in downtown Oslo, lined with chestnut trees. The distance from the school down to the tram was short, but the distance from the tram stop up to our house was infinite, up the long footpath at the north side of Stensparken with stairs at the end, me carrying a heavy satchel.

I did not walk the path alone. I was a child who was both seldom alone and often alone. Alone in the classroom while the other children went outside into the cold air, alone with my physiotherapist while the other children had gym class. But always alone with *an adult*, the physiotherapist, the school assistant, the orthopedist. These adults were responsible for caring for a boy, who, according to evaluations, would . . .

Clinical note, June 15, 1994 . . . *require significant additional assistance and follow-up both from his parents and social service workers.*

In other words, these adults were responsible for seeing that things went as well for me as possible. Their task was to shield me from the worst. From a friendly perspective, Social Services was made up of *good helpers*, but I found it difficult back then to see things from such a friendly perspective, and I still do.

Social Services wanted to serve, but they were not serviceable: I had to carry my satchel by myself even if it tired me out, because it was a good thing to get tired out, it was good exercise.

I went to the physiotherapist to have my arms and legs stretched, because it was good for me to be stretched until it hurt to ensure that the contractures in my muscles wouldn't grow worse. This was the 1980s. The principles from *then* do not apply *now*.

I was an indignant child. I am indignant still. This was the source of my indignation back then: someone else knew best. Near-stranger adults, the presence of whom I cannot shake off of me. This is still the source of my indignation: intentions I am unable to call good, unable to accept as anything other than a desire for power, desire to control. I was a child who was almost never alone.

To be a child is to be blind to one's self, it is to be unfettered in the world. To exist in the eyes of others is to be visible. Having to see one's self from the outside is having to gain control over one's self.

What has a child been *doing* all day long? *Nothing.* That is the answer to the adults' question. For this reason, a child cannot do *nothing* while adults are looking on. One cannot do *nothing* under the gaze of another person, an adult person.

The gaze of others is disciplinary.

The gaze of others, the adult gaze, makes time more visible. The time from here to there. The time between the hours, the school hours. A minute of spare time becomes a minute of waiting, several minutes of waiting. Walk back and forth between the desk and the wall, pull a book off the shelf. Sit down at the desk. Stare out the window. The minutes pass, though they do not seem to. Dream of being unfettered in the world. Dream of being free.

Am I romanticizing things now? Are there perhaps children somewhere in the world who do not seem to notice when adults are looking on, who live blissfully, unrestricted?

Of course, I am romanticizing things. I am writing about what I dreamt of then, and what

I still dream about today: absolute freedom of movement. Away from the restrictions of language, away from the restrictions of the body.

I sometimes gained admittance to this room, every now and then. For me, it is a concrete space, an experience, like being immersed in water.

Every Saturday, my family and I went to Berg Gård, a community center on the outskirts of north Oslo. There was a heated swimming pool in the basement, and Saturday morning was our time to visit this swimming pool, to be absolutely free.

In the pool, I did not have to worry about falling; in the pool, I did not have to worry about being clumsy. I was not a good swimmer, but I mastered a kind of doggy paddle. I am still a master at this technique. I hope I never fall into the ocean, but I feel intuitively at home immersed in calm, heated water. In the pool at Berg Gård, I was light enough to jump, strong enough to stand on one foot, lithe enough to spin. There, I could be free.

Once I began attending school, I would go to this pool while the others went to gym class, and then these visits took on another tone. I was not the only child who was driven to the swimming pool in a minibus. There were other students too, children from the special ed classes, children who were *really* different. Not different like me; these children drooled and shouted and lashed out. Children who I could not be like, I couldn't possibly be like them, no one could think that I was like them, could they? This was a new form of indignation, and a new form of moral experience.

Even one who is weak may despise weakness.

Rosemarie Garland-Thomson *The struggle for starees is how to look back.*

California is a space, a time, an arena where I learned a new language. I first traveled there in 2005, and have since returned several times because it is a space I can go to think, a space where I am able to envision myself.

I began to get a glimpse of which *we* I was a part of. Rosemarie Garland-Thomson writes about the paradoxically shared experience of being different. Those of us who stand out *are* a we, and we know it.

When I first wrote about these things, I was a research fellow. I wanted to understand myself, but from a safe distance. I leaned on academic language, academic categories.

I found common ground, fellowship, among interviews I conducted with people from a variety of different associations, people with very different bodies, different problems, different illnesses. They knew who they were in the world, and who resembled them. One of them said, "No one *wants* to know about this, about this side of reality." But some of us don't have a choice. We see the gaze of others directed toward us.

Mark O'Brien was a wheelchair user until he died; I am still a wheelchair user, and will be for as long as I live. We had our weakness in common. To be weak is to be subjected to the will of something else, of another person, or of an institution, but it is also to be *visible* to the other, to be, as they say, subject to another's gaze. This is what Rosemarie Garland-Thomson writes about when she writes about *staring*.

To be stared at, gawked at, is to develop an external sense of one's self, a sense that is always premodulated to the expectations of the surroundings. It is also to be situated in a narrative that has already been written, and that is told by others.

Mark O'Brien was stricken with polio. One coincidence was to be born before the polio vaccine was widely developed. My muscular disease is the result of another coincidence, which is itself the result of variations in the human genome. Life is also this.

There was no way of predicting it in 1981, the year I was born, not in the way that things are predicted today. Some conditions hidden in the genome can be identified. As I write this, an old dream has come one step closer to reality, the dream of cutting the mutations out of an embryo by editing its genetic code, a process not unlike the way I have edited this text. At the same time, life is unpredictable, mutations occur spontaneously; from a certain angle, it is precisely this unpredictability that *is* life. *There is grandeur in this view of life,* wrote Charles Darwin. I am mutating the meaning behind his words, ever so slightly, I am attempting to make them my own.

The consequences of the two conditions, the viral sickness and the genetic sickness, both fall into the category of physical weakness. The medical gaze, the genetic gaze, the clinical gaze: all perceive clear differences between these conditions. The world, on the other hand, does not. The world perceives a body with frail arms, legs locked into certain angles, the world sees a thin body in a large, bulky wheelchair. I surprise whenever I stand up, I shock when I take a step. Aren't all wheelchair users paralyzed from the waist down, what miracle is this?

It is not that easy. No pathological picture resembles another one perfectly. Diagnosis is not fate. But it's easy to believe that it is. It's easier not to look too closely. What *is* this gaze, which is so sharp and penetrating, but simultaneously dull and disinterested, that separates things that should not be separated and at the same time mistakes one thing for something very different?

I cannot step outside myself, I cannot fully become the normality that stares at difference. But I can try. And in the attempt something else might arise, something unpredictable. I wish to know who I no longer am, what country I've left, so that I can understand where I find myself now, which course I have set. I would like to know who I was expected to be, in order to more clearly see who I became.

Gaze and power share a long history. Rosemarie Garland-Thomson writes in the tradition of Foucault, who described the institutional gaze, the clinical gaze, and what happens to those of us who are subjected to such scrutiny.

In science fiction films and space operas, the enemy ship has a *tractor beam*, a ray of light that shoots out and immobilizes, captures. The flying saucer then pulls in the captivated object; experiments commence soon thereafter. I have to remind myself that this is an image, a metaphor. This might be because I myself have been a cybernetic organism, a cyborg, in the expanded sense of the word, from the time I got my first wheelchair. Between my organic body and the machine in which I maneuver myself every day there is a blurry line, my pulse quickens whenever something or someone bumps into the wheelchair, it is an instinctive reaction. It requires little effort on my part to see the reality in stories where other people see pure fantasy and wild thought experiments.

Institutions stare at individuals, subjecting them to their control. Foucault's most popular image, employed to illustrate this control, this surveillance, was borrowed from Jeremy

Bentham, the father of utilitarianism. It is the panopticon.

In the panopticon, which was supposedly Bentham's idea of the perfect prison system, guards sit at the hub of a large, circular structure with an uninhibited view of the cells comprising the wheel. The prisoners never know when they are being observed and therefore must adapt all of their behavior *as if they are always being observed*. This is the central point. The gaze is ceaselessly disciplinary. It steers the body's conduct via the mind. One knows that one is being watched, therefore one behaves as one should. This was the disciplinary model for the prison system of the 1800s, it is the model for our school systems today, as well as for countless other institutions.

I was not an institutionalized child. No more so than any other kindergarten or primary school child. However, I was constantly in contact with institutions that do not exist for everyone. I have memories of being examined by doctors and physiotherapists. I am six, seven, eight years old in these memories, in rooms that are a little too cold, in my underwear. Someone is touching the muscles of my arms and legs. I am instructed to walk from one end of the room, turn, and walk back. I know that I am being observed, I don't know why. Then my parents and I go home.

There is something strangely fragmentary and particular about these episodes, these memories, they don't have the same fluid, timeless quality as other memories from my childhood, at home, or at the cabin, in which countless days, all of them resembling one another, have blended and blurred together, have become images rooted to a place that grows fuzzy around the edges, in which everything that happens takes place over the course of one single, eternal summer's day.

In the medical memories, *kairos* and *kronos* have switched places. The moment is located outside of time, held fast and fixed there with steel surgical clips, whereas the ordinary everyday, a child's ordinary everyday, is infused with presence and links to the whole. This part of my childhood, by far the largest part, remains protected.

I ask my parents how much effort it was to have a child like me. They take their time before responding to this question in particular. They prefer talking about other efforts. "I was practically the caretaker," my father says with regard to the subdivided Swiss villa where we owned one of the three apartments. In 1979, they were given the Architecture Protection Prize by the local chapter of the National Trust for their renovation of the building. They were—they are—a team of workers, and I have inherited their work ethic.

We may speak about what is and what was difficult. But first we have to be certain that everything is all right. Only now, when I am here, in my life, having become a father myself, are we able to say, aloud and in chorus: *It was difficult.*

This formulation is a gross understatement, but we do not say anything more dramatic than that. It's not our way. There's a Calvinistic streak running through our family, as through many Norwegian families. Nor is it wise to say that everything has gone well; nothing in this world lasts forever. One may create something good if one works at it, one may create a refuge for a short while.

Mine was a sheltered childhood, with small, piercing stabs of another reality poking in. What I do not yet know is why I experience the distance between these two realities as so great. It was always me, all the time; all the time, I had my body.

I did not stop having a congenital muscle disease whenever I left the consultation room; I never got a vacation from my wheelchair. Our cabin had a ground-level root cellar where we stored the wheelchair at night. Whenever I parked it outside my friends' houses, or outside shops, I was reminded of tying up a dog; I felt guilty if I forgot that I'd parked it there. The foreign elements did not exist in my ordinary, day-to-day life. They came from outside.

Within the health-care system, the modern clinic, a human being is observed analytically, with regard to their basic and generic parts. Premodern illness was personal and intimate, a consequence of an individual's temperament and life situation, it was a holistic variable that had to be handled holistically. Not surprisingly, doctors killed at least as many patients as they saved.

The modern clinic was contrived as a place for gathering knowledge about illnesses and diagnoses. Like would no longer be treated with like, indiscriminately; rather, ultimate causes would be sought. And the diseases became more important, perhaps more real, than the individual patients. The same ailments would be given equal treatment, regardless of whether the one suffering was an aristocrat or tenant farmer, a man from Lyon or a woman from Louisville.

It is in the crosshairs of these two gazes—the controlling institutional gaze and the penetrating clinical gaze—that we find ourselves, Mark O'Brien and I. Is it therefore so strange that we learned early on to despise our bodies, with their weaknesses and vulnerabilities?

That which is seen and put into words suppresses something else that remains nameless, but nonetheless does not cease to exist. It is hard to be human beneath the institutional gaze, for what the institution does not see, it does not acknowledge. In England in the 1960s and 1970s, young people, some of whom had been institutionalized for as long and as unwillingly as O'Brien, began to fight for their rights. The movement focused at first on issues of money and power, and access to jobs. A generation would pass before it addressed intimacy and sexuality, issues that required a private room, a space in which the most vulnerable mysteries could be explored.

I think I know why it took so long. I think I can recognize the need to fight on solid ground, to not make oneself more vulnerable than one must. I think I recognize the need to show that one is *just as good* in at least one arena, to show what one is good for, that it's just that the rules of play are unfair. I think I am writing about myself in order to understand the world, and that for many years I wanted to make myself as invulnerable as possible, in order to pose undeniable claims.

I still feel this impulse in myself. I want everything to be *just so*. I want to know my rights. At the same time, I am increasingly curious about areas in which *rights* is the wrong word, where reason falls short. When I first read Mark O'Brien, I was very uncomfortable. He is my shadow for many reasons, but the most important reason is that he put into words a form of corporeal self-loathing that I could scarcely admit to knowing.

O'Brien wrote, in his essay "On Seeing a Sex Surrogate," about his deep-rooted conviction, his fear, that *someone who was not an attendant, nurse, or doctor would be horrified at seeing my pale, thin body with its bent spine, bent neck, washboard ribcage, and hipbones protruding like outriggers . . .*

This is a painful paragraph to read because he has taken on the clinical language; he examines himself with a clinical gaze, body part by body part, deformity by deformity. Is there any human body that does not appear repugnant under this gaze?

O'Brien's essay was meant to provoke; it describes his first sexual experience with another person, a woman who offered these kinds of sexual experiences to carefully selected clients for payment. The essay was also about vulnerability and finding peace, about a form of self-acceptance, and his essay was often read in this light, it is still read in this light by many.

I read it with a completely different sense of unease, since it was about something that I have always feared the most: the lack of genuine intimacy. I shrank from regarding the vulnerability too closely, and not only that, I shrank from regarding too closely any of what O'Brien revealed, the discomfort that he laid bare, for I was able to sense myself in it. When it came right down to it, he had paid for sex. Should that be considered a revolution and a victory, to use the words *sex surrogate* as a therapeutic term, a displacement of discourse in which the body becomes a commodity just like everything else? Would I have done the same thing if I had felt a little lonelier, a little more isolated from social circles, and would I have explained myself, excused my choice with clinical language, the clinical gaze?

One day, I was invited to sit on a discussion panel at Rockefeller, a rock venue in Oslo. They were going to screen a film, *The Sessions*, based on Mark O'Brien's essay, or, perhaps, to put it more precisely, based on the experiences that provided the basis for his essay. That there was a film version was strange in itself, for how could one believably cast the part of O'Brien? His body was unique. How many actors are there who have had polio and weigh less than a twelve-year-old child?

The actor they found, John Hawkes, is five-foot-nine, according to IMDb, the Internet Movie Database. And his weight must be at least three times that of O'Brien's. They got around this by filming as little as possible of the actor's body, concentrating the camera on his head. This is how they were able to create the illusion, after a fashion. In this way, he lay without moving; in this way, he spoke with his limited lung capacity.

The film was nominated for an Oscar, as films of this type often are, as an acknowledgment of the *intimate* and *vulnerable* and *universal*, which isn't universal at all, since O'Brien's experiences were so special that they were foreign to me as well. I cannot and should not be allowed to identify with him or to invoke his victimhood for myself. His vulnerability was extreme, and when an extreme life experience is made into a *story*, there is also the risk that the storyteller, even if she is the very person to whom it happened, might exercise violence toward the experience itself. Wittgenstein wrote about the impossibility of a private language for emotions; to cloak something in words is to adapt it to the expectations of one's listeners and readers, to their world.

Nevertheless, films like *The Sessions* touch on something that can masquerade as universal, and that permits the organizations and interest groups to see their part in things: now we will discuss the basic human right to intimacy, now we are going to talk about laws about prostitution, about everything that is *problematic* and *challenging*. To such organizations and groups, I am a person with a name, I have a relevant doctoral degree, and I am asked to appear on discussion panels and find myself unable to say no.

I don't want to show up, but it feels like I don't have a choice. My sense of obligation is so overpowering that it doesn't need to announce itself. It is discursively controlling, in Foucault's sense: it defines the terms by which it is possible to think, possible to speak, possible to act. Obligation has always created these relationships in advance so that I don't even have to make a decision; things are positioned in such a way that I do what must be done. I often can't sleep the night before such engagements, before traveling to the remote place where I don't want to be, to deliver a lecture in that remote place, to attend the unpleasant conference there. My body rebels, but the sense of obligation wins. How else could I have become *someone*?

Ida still cannot understand the source of my antagonism, though she encountered it soon enough. Once she has inhabited this space too, she is able to understand my irrational fear, the fear that I will never be able to leave the venue again. In a scene from Tod Browning's 1932 film *Freaks*, the misshapen carnival performers raise their chant in repellent chorus, in nightmarish clarity: *Gooble, gobble . . . one of us, one of us!*

At the panel discussion about *The Sessions*, there are too many shadows in the room, too few bodies. At first, Ida can't comprehend the negation, why the conversation remains so abstract and distant. In *this* hall, full of wheelchairs and walkers, after the screening of a film *like that*, it's still only possible to talk about sex and intimacy as fundamental variables, as a topic for parliamentary reports and public inquiries. We have watched and seen the vulnerability, but we shy away, we are unable to speak of it.

Afterward, we're talking with the other panelists and friends who came to hear me speak. That's when Ida realizes that she is not my girlfriend, not for some of those speaking with us. I am sitting in my wheelchair, she is standing beside me, and this means that she is an assistant, hired to help me with my *daily activities*, so now it is her nightmare that is coming true, not mine.

There are living assistants in attendance, at Rockefeller, and none of them are introduced by name. What *is* said, more than once, is: *This is my arms and legs*, and this is meant to be humorous, it is a political assertion, those who say it believe they are being progressive. *No!* Ida wants to shout. *You have your own arms and legs! And that is a human being standing there next to you, and I am another human being, and this person in the wheelchair is my boyfriend!*

And my first impulse is to say: *Please don't make a scene. This isn't the time, this isn't the place.* But now *is* precisely the time and the place to speak openly, to avoid the misleading metaphors. These are people who require services and receive them, the way I have received them, albeit only under certain conditions, from a Social Services system that principally shuts feelings out, that only relates to what is essential and sufficient. The *arms and legs* are included as part of a metaphor suited to the idea of such an apparatus, a surrogate metaphor, in which the substitution can never be as good as the original. The surrogate legs cross the floor, the surrogate arms pick up the newspaper, surrogate partners offer a substitute for intimacy.

Ida and I are a couple out with other couples. We are just like the others. We are nothing like the others. She is my first real girlfriend, there is so much that is new for me, but *I* am not in doubt about who we are to each other. This doubt comes from outside.

And yet, two realities pulsate side by side. I still identify strongly with Mark O'Brien, in his books, in the film, but I have begun to live a life that is radically different from his. I have begun to let go of something, and as I release it, I am in a better position to recognize it, to put into words what for so long has been nothing but an all-consuming, bodily experience.

The clinical gaze creates *subjects*, Foucault writes, who are subjected to it as such, but not *objects*, and inherent in this distinction is a moral burden and a mandate for the person observed. The subject always has a self-narrative, she is an active party and learns to believe that her actions are her own, thus the subject comes to believe that she alone bears the responsibility for the situation in which she finds herself. Subjugation is an assignment of responsibility without self-determination, resulting in the internalization of guilt, which then becomes shame.

Michel Foucault *He who is subjected to a field of visibility, and who knows it, assumes responsibility for the constraints of power; he makes them play spontaneously upon himself; he inscribes in himself the power relation in which he simultaneously plays both roles; he becomes the principle of his own subjection.*

It can be surprisingly hard to imagine a form of resistance to such a gaze that does not require the subjugation of another, a reduction of the other to their body parts, to arms and legs, to a supporting role. I am familiar with this kind of rhetoric, I am able to understand it, but with each passing year such thinking feels more and more foreign to me.

The term *sex surrogate* is a part of this rhetoric. It aims to transcend the clinical and counteract institutional power, but it does so by imitating the neutral, instrumental language of the institution. It is a rhetoric that intends to give control—and thereby also freedom, identity, and autonomy—to the powerless. Those unable to walk themselves may now borrow someone else's legs; those who cannot move their arms may now steer another's arms.

If the battle cannot be won in this way, it is partly because the language employed carries with it too many traces of the original. The dictionary demonstrates this best: a *surrogate* is a *(bad) substitute*, a *replacement*, often when an object has been worn out, and what is it that we are calling an object, *who* are we calling an object? But another reason is that such language undermines the value of the only thing that actually exists, namely, the body that is in fact present in the world, that is irreplaceable, precisely because to replace it would be to eliminate it.

Resistance therefore must come from another quarter, for by using the language of surrogacy, one becomes trapped inside a pocket of reality, a shadow landscape in which the dish being served is always wartime fare of chicory and bark bread, and war is the normal state of being, it is a war without end. Within this pocket, this shadow reality, everyday life is simulated as if the reality outside is so far out of reach that only a pale substitute will suffice. One only speaks openly about replacements, substitutes, surrogates when reality and authenticity are considered unattainable.

Social Services constantly churns out such language, with their well-intentioned expressions of *meaningful follow-up*, of *supporting the subject*, whose quality of life must be measured in negatives, whose life, under the best conditions, can only be brought close to a zero-balance, who is given the label *well-functioning*. After a few decades of being the *subject* of Social Services, this *(bad) substitute* for a dream can seem enticing; it might even be mistaken for a purpose.

✣ ✣ ✣

It's two months after the panel discussion at Rockefeller. Ida and I are in California, we are staying there for a month, and this month I am writing most of what is going to be a book called *Body Language, Kroppsspråk* in Norwegian. I am still much more preoccupied by language than body at this point. The title is there long before the book has found its form, which is what happens sometimes.

In California, in Berkeley, we are sitting outside, it's March, it's sixty-eight degrees, and the spring air wafting from the Pacific is sharp and clear, we are in the elevated back garden of the Imperial Tea Court on Shattuck Avenue. At regular intervals, the kitchen exhales a whiff of deep-fried dim sum, but they have the spicy chili ginger beer that Ida likes, and we can sit there writing for hours while the schoolchildren buy ice cream in one of the shops downstairs, whooping ecstatically.

The building is decorated with Asian details here and there, on the ceilings, in the doorways, but is wide enough and sturdy enough to withstand earthquakes. The ramp up to the terrace where we are seated is a gentle, even slope, most of the buildings here are wheelchair assessible, and there is a beam on the side where children can balance and stretch their arms out to reach for the palm trees, or the flowers with their explosive colors, or the sky. The sunshine is strong and clear and burns hotter as the day progresses, burning off the fog coming in from the ocean, and we don't say much, but we lift our eyes every now and then, to smile at each other, to acknowledge that we are here, that we are us, that this day is perfectly aligned with our view of things.

The next morning, we get up again in the daylight-basement apartment that we are renting on Edith Street, an apartment that we chose because it didn't have any steps up to the entrance, and because there was a covered space to park the wheelchair, it rains in Northern California in March, but it doesn't rain the month that we are there, the acute drought that the state is experiencing offers us an unconstrained, timeless vacation away from reality in Norway, and from every kind of gaze. We make our breakfast with yogurt, granola, and honey, and the enormous blueberries that we buy at the Monterey Market. We make coffee with Berkeley tap water, it never tastes fantastic, but still it is a nice ritual. We walk slowly up along Cedar Street and find our writing spot where we stay until it's time to shop for dinner, we share a bottle of wine, we go to bed at the same time. The next morning, we start the whole thing over.

Each of us is writing our own book, books that are about what is most difficult for us, mine is about body and language, Ida's is about her family history, and we write under the California sun, where the time difference and distance from Norway makes it possible to see things more clearly than usual, as clear as the sharp spring air. Mark O'Brien lived here too; he lived what was his life and not a surrogate life.

It could have been different. It always could have been different. But who would I have been if I hadn't been born with a muscular disease? There is a lived life and there is an unlived life, and the lived life contains the unlived one as water contains an air bubble.

I received a diagnosis of spinal muscular atrophy when I was three years old. I can scarcely remember the period of time before I thought of myself as *someone who had a muscular disease*, but it is a brief opening before something else, a door, a lock, bang.

I was able to walk, but not run. I was able to stand up from the floor, but only if I had something to hold on to for support. Outside, where the ground was uneven, I needed the wheelchair. The wheelchair was freedom, from tripping, from falling, from exhaustion.

None of this was new. It had always been this way. I was always already myself. Any uncertainty was about who I wanted to become. My diagnosis described a so-called progressive condition, in other words, we could assume that it was going to get worse. Or, as was stated in the papers from the time I was thirteen:

Clinical note, June 15, 1994

Spinal muscular atrophy, type II–III with some reduction of physical proficiencies over the past years in correlation with growth, nonetheless fairly stable.

[...]

Otherwise gets along well with a combination of manual wheelchair, power wheelchair, and lifting seat to get out of deeper chairs.

[...]

Good intellectual and social functionality but will require significant extra support and follow-up in future years both from his parents and social service workers.

It's strange to see one's self described in such terms, but this is the language of these notes, this is the language of clinics and institutions. It is as much directed toward the future as it is the present, and the future is bleak. In this language, each and every positive notation is temporary and cautious. The language of clinics and institutions is the language of depression, expecting little and hoping for even less.

My relationship to these future projections was unclear. When you are thirteen, the thought of someday being twenty and no longer able to walk feels as remote as it is fatalistic. What difference did it make whether I exercised and went to my physiotherapist if my muscles were going to waste away in any case? What else could I do besides go to class?

There is a theory that depressed people are more realistic than others; they see the world as it is.

The world is full of the trivial, the petty, this applies to everyone, but it's worst when you require help. Social Services can work no magic, it is an old, rickety apparatus that regularly breaks down. Social Services doesn't pick up the phone, it publishes studies, it switches jobs, it sometimes doesn't show up. Social Services is ambitious, it stretches out its skinny fists like antennas to the sky.

I began to write because I needed a different language than the one I was offered.

In his commencement speech at the Collège de France, Michel Foucault lectured about the word that exists before one's attempts to grasp and steer it, before one founders and discovers that, instead, one has been led astray, that the word enslaves.

❖ ❖ ❖

I wish I could have slipped surreptitiously into this discourse which I must present today, and into the ones I shall have to give here, perhaps for many years to come. **Michel Foucault**

❖ ❖ ❖

It is and it isn't like this. I don't wish to slip surreptitiously into the discourse I present here, I want rather to push it along, I want to feel the sweat and toil as I carry out this task. This book cannot begin until I have found its language, and by the time the language exists, the book will be finished, all of the work will be done.

I write this beneath the weight of all the records, the magazine boxes and binders full of papers that my parents gave me. They are stacked behind me in the office, projecting their gravitational field. What these papers tell is something far away, like stars, their rays have reached me. I am trying to figure out how much or how little they are able to say about my childhood—not the way I experienced it, the way it was shaped in my memories, but as viewed through another lens, an external lens.

When Ida and I were getting to know each other, it was not these papers that we talked about. Our intimacy did not increase because we discussed case notes and letters of complaint and legal documents. These papers have nothing to say about the things I remember as true. And yet, by virtue of their duration, they are both more reliable and more stable than my own memory. They compete with the photographs in albums that I keep on my bookshelves at home, those typical photographs from a 1980s childhood, though several of the photos are untypically good since my father was and is a skilled photographer, and many of them are also untypical because of objects that recur throughout, such as the wheelchair.

It is a temptation to think that I am writing myself *beyond* the clinical notes, deeper in toward a true kernel of experience. We always want the truth, be it the poetic or the biographical, to be located at the center.

Yet my childhood experiences of the world were often suffused with mystery and confusion. For example: the red house where we lived, my parents, sister, and I, was a Swiss-style villa. We lived in the second-floor unit. On the stair landings between the floors and on the bottom floor there were stalls that used to be privies, back when the night-soil men came to empty them. Every time I climbed the stairs slowly, straining from step to step, leaning in toward the banister to find the point where I could lay my weight, I wondered how this system had worked. Weren't the people who used the privy on the bottom floor afraid of getting hit in the head by the occupants of the toilets above them?

The high school senior party bus parked at the neighbor's house was another mystery. A red box truck with white lettering on one side: HOW DO YOU TRICK A JUNIOR INTO WALKING AROUND A BUS A HUNDRED TIMES? ANSWER ON THE OPPOSITE SIDE. I thought long and hard about this joke but couldn't figure it out. That was the kind of kid I was. And these were the types of questions I pondered at length back then, these were life's greatest mysteries until I became more self-aware, until I had a stronger sense of who I was.

✤ ✤ ✤

Erving Goffman The sociologist Erving Goffman writes about stigma, about the *discrediting visual marker*. In ancient Greece, where the word originates, a stigma was branded on the skin. It signaled to all good citizens that *this* person was not a person, they were a runaway slave, property gone astray. This is someone without a place in the *polis*, in the life of the city. *Don't speak with the marked one, don't have anything to do with the marked one. The marked one does not require respect.* This is not a person, it is a *bare life*, unprotected.

A stigma is always a visible marker on the body. Needle marks on the forearms. Damaged teeth. Thin, stringy hair on a chafed scalp. A lurch in one's gait, staggering. A body unable to walk properly, that requires a wheelchair to move around.

The stigmas vary, but they are alike in the reactions they engender. They engender small theatrical productions. The other actors immediately comprehend the scene that has been set in motion. They veer off, they look away. If the scene nonetheless ends in eye contact, this is a provocation, a confrontation. Someone has crossed a line.

Stigma is contagious. It has an expansive and flexible aura. Not only is it able to surround an entire body, it can also be spread to other bodies. It can eat itself from the outside in, it can form a personality, it can form the conditions, both with regard to itself and with regard to others, that in turn form personalities of their own. It is only a matter of time.

The point in the protected individual's life when the domestic circle can no longer protect him will vary by social class, place of residence, and type of stigma, but in each case will give rise to a moral experience when it occurs.

Erving Goffman

A moral experience. Yes. For me, it came late, since I came from a social situation in which my home circle was so wide that it was easy to confuse it with society as a whole, or even the world. Nevertheless, the moral experience, just as Goffman writes, consisted of a loss of protection. What I felt was the indignation over the loss of certain privileges, or, as it might be better stated, over discovering that others enjoyed physical privileges that I have never had and never will have.

This discovery was delayed for a long time. When I started school, my mother accompanied me to my classroom, all of the children gathered around her and she gave them a little presentation. She showed how easy it was for me to fall, and she explained that it was not kind to push me roughly. And I never was pushed, from what I can remember, neither at primary school nor in junior high. That was another kind of moral experience, though it took several years before I appreciated it. I first had to become acquainted with someone else who had been bullied, for I certainly never was. Among the other children, I was safe. The circle was wide.

✦ ✦ ✦

From the earliest period:

The boy has clinical signs of neuromuscular illness, presum-
ably myopathy which seems to affect all muscular areas.

Clinical note,
June 12, 1984

His parents are of course interested in the quickest pos-
sible explanation. I am sending him, with his parents'
consent, for sampling in the children's clinic.

"Quickest possible explanation"; well-chosen
words, optimistic words, unrealistic words. It was
only recently, after turning thirty, that I received a
diagnosis that I'm able to believe I'll have for the
rest of my life. It felt like putting on a tailored
suit for the first time, a garment specifically measured to my body and not to the average body.

The explanation that my parents received in the
1980s was temporary. It indicated a life different than the one I have lived. According to
that explanation, I should not have been able
to go out in my twenties. I should have been
weaker. My ankles should have been operated
on around the age of twelve. This *should have been*

was at the forefront of the clinical language. The clinical language suggests another world.

A few years ago, my best friend had a son. He started school. In his curriculum plan, the curriculum plan for a six-year-old boy, it stated the expectation that he should be able to draw the school building from the front, in perspective, and that he should be able to explain what the Humanist Association is. It also stated, under the category Physical Education, the expectation that he should be able to run.

I shouldn't take it personally. I should know that all of the bulleted points in the curriculum plan are absurd when read sequentially. It's no more preposterous to act as if a six-year-old's running abilities can be measured than it is to pretend that the child will be able to comprehend and explain what the Humanist Association is. But I do take it personally, on behalf of all of the children who were never able to run, who will never be able to run.

It's only now, now that schools have become total institutions, that the normalizing norm is so strikingly visible. In the weekly plan for a six-year-old boy, it states, both descriptively and normatively at once: *I can run.* I don't happen to know, today, any six-year-old boys who are unable to run. But I know they exist, and I know something about how they are experiencing the world.

He will soon be 7 years old. Height is in the 50th percentile and weight is 19.8 kilos (surprising, as he appeared to be much lighter). I think he suffers from a more generally diffuse muscular atrophy and obvious myopathic facies.
[. . .]
Preparations should be made to start school, he has taught himself to read (after intensive independent study for 3 weeks) and can already do a fair bit with numbers.

Clinical note, March 10, 1988

With these words, I take a step forward: a soon-to-be seven-year-old child with a congenital muscular disease. Who is interested in Legos and cartoons, and soon also books by Tolkien, the role-playing of Dungeons & Dragons, and strategy games, whether board games or on the

PC; a child who, *after intensive independent study*, has begun to understand what it is to read and write.

In *Wings of Desire*, the narrator reads a poem by Peter Handke, "Song of Childhood":

Als das Kind Kind war,
ging es mit hängenden Armen,
wollte der Bach sei ein Fluß,
der Fluß sei ein Strom,
und diese Pfütze das Meer.

Als das Kind Kind war,
wußte es nicht, daß es Kind war,
alles war ihm beseelt,
und alle Seelen waren eins.
[. . .]
Als das Kind Kind war,
hatte es von nichts eine Meinung,
hatte keine Gewohnheit,
saß oft im Schneidersitz,
lief aus dem Stand,
hatte einen Wirbel im Haar
und machte kein Gesicht beim Fotografieren.

The words linger inside of me, in spite of my limited understanding. Me, with my spotty knowledge of German and Dutch. Bruno Ganz's voice as he recites *Wings of Desire* is melodic, melancholic. I search for a translation:

When the child was a child,
it walked with arms hanging,
wanted the creek to be a river,
the river to be a torrent,
and this puddle, the sea.

When the child was a child,
it did not know it was a child,
everything to him was filled with soul,
and all souls were one.
[...]
When the child was a child,
it had no opinion on things,
no habits,
sat mostly cross-legged,
leapt into a run,
a cowlick in its hair,
made no faces when photographed.

This particular child did not leap into a run, he could not sit cross-legged, but he was still the same child, and when I swam my movements were free, and I made no faces.

The protective circle of the family ends where the institutional landscape begins. The one does not envelop the other, not completely, but it can be difficult to see past the high walls, with their sharp corners and straight edges.

I cannot know how it must have felt to be *close* to this child, to be his parents, to be his social workers. But now that I have a son too, this role is closer to me now than that of the child from back then. This is also a moral experience.

Doctor's note, undated *Jan Grue is so severely physically disabled due to muscular disease that he will require extra assistance from the start of his schooling. The muscular disease cannot be expected to improve and there will be many issues to consider throughout the school day, during both the lessons and recess.*

Many issues *would* have to be considered. The extra assistants accompanied me from the time I started going to school so that the necessary considerations could be taken. I was allowed to stay in during recess, the assistants followed me around the school, they followed wherever I walked or wheeled. That was one way of taking things into consideration.

I did not do well with this arrangement. I was indignant. However, I lacked an object toward which to direct my indignation, I lacked an outlet, I did not understand *why*, even if I had long ago come to understand that a different set of rules applied to me than to others.

The psychoanalyst D. W. Winnicott poses a question that is just as good as it is impossible to answer: *What is the normal child?*

The question does not have any answers without a context. The child does not exist in isolation; it is surrounded by family; the family is surrounded by society.

The purely logical answer is, in itself, a double negation: the normal child is the child who *is not deviant.* There are a thousand ways to deviate from the norm. We don't notice it until we are made aware of it, but then shame enters the picture. Shame over not being like the others. The shame of standing out, the shame of being a nuisance.

This shame continues to show up today, it bangs loudly at my door every time a place, a building, is not wheelchair accessible. Once, I went to the city center to shop for kitchen chairs. The store had an elevator inside, as is often the case with stores, but it was being used as a storage space, as also is often the case with stores. I ruffled up my sense of irritation over this tiny, trivial hindrance—irritation is a safe feeling—and called down the stairs to the staff, requesting that they clear out the elevator. The red flush of shame on my cheeks was a purely physiological reaction; I *know* there's nothing for me to be ashamed of, that no one had done anything with malice, that no one had intentionally meant to bar me from entering the store. I *know* this, now.

✣ ✣ ✣

One episode that is not immortalized on paper, which has not been described in any note or letter: I am in fourth grade, and there is a birthday party for one of the girls. Everyone is invited. It is winter. We are out on a local playground, which is right next to the school. We have had snow this winter. At the center of the playground is a large field covered over with a sheet of ice.

The other children are ice-skating. I figure out that I can use my wheelchair as a sled. I start by driving very fast, slam on the brakes, and off I go, gliding across the ice, spinning around once, twice, three times. It's entirely friction-free, and then it turns magical. Someone hitches onto the wheelchair, grabs the basket behind the seat. I continue driving, pulling them along. A tail of children cobbles onto the wheelchair, grows longer. They are drawn toward me from around the courtyard, like iron filings to a magnet.

From above, the movement on the ice must look like something gentle and strange and beautiful. Ten years later, I go to a film school in Denmark and watch Busby Berkeley's perfectly synchronized choreography in *Footlight Parade*. It takes me a while to understand what I am seeing. What I remember.

Stephin Merritt   *We still dance on whirling stages*
in my Busby Berkeley Dreams

A wavelike movement of children, a broad spiral, for a brief moment a straight line, the next moment a new, swaying ribbon, and then a quiet and cautious click, and the wheelchair glides off again, to a stop. The little electric motor has reached its limit. The wheelchair will never wake up again.

The party is not over. We are all going to go to the birthday girl's house. I am driven there. The birthday girl's father has a motorcycle with a sidecar. We fly through the darkness.

According to Social Services:

Notice of
resolution,
December 17,
1996

Mobility aids are the property of the national social security system and as such are considered borrowed goods.

Such devices may not be sold, exchanged, given away, loaned out, borrowed, or pawned. Proper care must be taken of aid devices to avoid unnecessary wear and tear / depreciation of value. With regards.

Out on the ice in fourth grade, I experienced a form of freedom that was different than freedom in the swimming pool. Even in the wheelchair, it was possible to move without thinking about *how* I moved, without fear of falling. By the time I was in seventh grade, the wheelchair had begun to feel like a part of my body. I especially noticed this when my class went for a one-week wilderness school. The bus only had room for a manual wheelchair. The kind of wheelchair I was not strong enough to propel myself, that had to be pushed by others. By the time I returned home at the end of the week, I was irritated and upset because it was the first time I had been *confined to a wheelchair*; this expression has a particular meaning for me.

The wilderness school was located in the mountain plateau region west of Oslo, called

Langedrag, and was surrounded by wild terrain. A family who owned wolves lived in Langedrag. It was a good base for excursions and outdoor experiences. The others went on hikes. I was pushed in circles around the lake on a wide, gently sloping path, around and around.

The electric wheelchair that I was used to didn't work well whenever a path became too narrow, or roots too knobby, but it still made the attempt. It pushed just as hard as I did. We wanted the same thing. The manual wheelchair, by contrast, was nothing but a chair on wheels. We could not work together. It could not do anything for me.

I was ten when we moved. I loved the red Swiss villa in Lyder Sagens gate, as did my sister, as did our parents. It became increasingly difficult for me to get up the stairs to the second floor. My wheelchair was parked down in the bicycle shed, and from there it was several paces over to the house. There were steps up to the entryway, where I could use the chair lift that we had installed. It sufficed. But it grew more and more difficult.

I was the kind of teenager who read about superheroes. I read myths. I played computer games. It was the 1990s, and computers were beige and gray, and processing power was measured as 286, 386, 486. I played the strategy game *Civilization*, and it gave meaning to the world around me. In the game, I ruled over an empire through vast periods of history, from antiquity to modernity.

That was a tidy, transparent world. The conflicts were understandable, the goals were clear. I aimed for the stars, the highest aim of the game being to send a spaceship to Alpha Centauri, to expand the scope of humanity on a new planet. This required thousands of years of hard work, targeted effort.

Whether unconsciously or consciously, I developed into a child who planned things, who *enjoyed* planning things. This characteristic is still quite prominent in me. I can no longer remember if I understood the reason why we had to move, but I know that I had already begun to think about the future.

Some historians believe that it is not until after the Middle Ages that a clear notion of *change*—of development, progression—was formulated. Hesiod wrote about decline, about the lost Golden Age and the Iron Age to come, but this was an interpretation of the laws of history. It was not an attempt to change them.

Decline is a given, be it in a body or in a civilization. The question is whether we believe there's anything that can be done about it, and if so—what?

Another memory, another moral experience, is from that same playground, in the summer. The memory is reduced, or distilled, to a still frame, its lesson is conveyed like a medieval tableau.

The tones in this memory are shame and rage and indignation. Down below, in the flat, dusty center of the playground, I am driving around, while the other boys are up on the green, grassy fringes. I want them to do something, there is something that *I* want that *they* don't want, and I understand that there is a chasm between us. They are up and able to come down to me, but they don't want to, and I am unable to go up to them, no matter how much I would like to. The truth is that my friends are free to go their own way at any time, to a place where I cannot follow.

This memory is so clear because it was reinforced, again and again, in the years that followed. Throughout my childhood and into my teen years, it became increasingly apparent to me that there were places that existed into which I could not enter, experiences to which I could gain no access. I was in constant contact with Terminus, the Roman god of boundaries and boundary markers. *What* these spaces were, I could not quite say; I dreamt of sex and booze and, above all, something hidden and unencumbered and secret, a place where control did not exist.

I was certain that everyone else knew about such places, that they were located at the top of a stairwell I wasn't strong enough to climb, at the end of a path that was too long and narrow for me to navigate. Perhaps I had an inkling that other teenagers might have similar feelings of exclusion, but I don't remember that now. Paradoxically enough, I have an empathetic but somewhat distant relationship to the youth that I was then, but I try remembering how he felt, I try edging closer to his experience.

I am met by a tiny emotional echo whenever a stairwell is too high, whenever a doorway is too narrow, a corner too sharp. An echo resonates whenever I have to get up alone and send my electric wheelchair away, whenever I have to sit down in a manual wheelchair and wait for support personnel. Whenever an airplane has arrived, and I've been left sitting alone in the cabin for an hour, as the cabin crew grows impatient, and still there's no sign of my wheelchair, that's when I know that all of the other passengers have already arrived at the parties they were going to, and I am left sitting alone with Terminus.

The great pendulum swings between the absent, this no-man's-land that I am offered, and the empty space that I create for myself. It is an exercise in exploration and discovery that takes a lifetime. I must think in a new way about the old. I must turn each word over. It is a large and detailed map I wish to draw.

One part of this map: wheelchairs have a cultural history and a technological history. It is a secret history. There is a viewpoint that one may establish, a particular awareness that one may exercise, and then the world is completely different. To tell a secret history, if it is about one's self, is to take back the world.

I was not old when I drove an electric wheelchair for the first time, the Permobil, with powerful rear-wheel drive and light blue body. I insist on this word: *drive*. One sits in a wheelchair when one is seated without moving, completely still. Another word I am able to concede: *ride*.

The Permobil tossed me out of the saddle once, in second grade, when I crashed into an apple tree. It was my fault, I didn't have control, I didn't respect the will of the beast. But I learned, I mastered the technique. This was finding my way in the world. I learned that there were circles outside the inner circle, and about the art of the possible.

The lever to give gas protruded up and out from the engine case on the left side. The lever had a knob I could grip, I had to extend my left arm forward to put the wheelchair in motion. I thought the lever resembled my elbow, both locked in forty-five-degree angles. On the right side was the lever for steering. To turn to the right, I had to pull it backward, to turn to the left, I had to push it forward. It was heavy, especially if the wheelchair was going slowly. The faster I went, the easier it was to turn.

As I write this today, the technology I am describing is as if from a different century. The physical experience of using a wheelchair like that is almost nonexistent these days. When I went to film school, the transition from analog to digital film editing was nearly complete. One experienced negative cutter spoke of the sensation of bringing the heavy blade down onto the physical strip of film, of having the rhythm of the film in one's body, of the knowledge that the moment is *now*.

On July 28, 1794, the tenth day of the Revolution of Thermidor, Georges Couthon was led to the guillotine. It was difficult to strap him down because of his contracted muscles.

Couthon's wheelchair is on display in Paris, at the Musée Carnavalet. It is obviously a converted lounge chair. It has upholstery, armrests, and carved decorations. There are two large wheels at the front and a small steering wheel at the back, and the truly remarkable thing is this: both of the front wheels each has a ring of bolts on the inside. Two primitive turning mechanisms are controlled by handles at the same height as the handrests.

In this way, Couthon was able to maneuver his chair on his own, if not without enormous effort. By turning one of the handles, he could turn around, and by turning both handles, in a

continuous motion, he could steer the wheelchair forward and backward.

It must have felt like carrying a full tank of
oil on your back, like pulling a car with your
teeth. The wheels were made of solid wood, the
driving gears were handmade. This wheelchair
would have been impossible to use outdoors,
on cobblestones, in muddy streets.

I can understand why he had it built, I can
understand why it was important. I can identify, have sympathy. With enormous effort,
he was able to turn the chair around to see
who had addressed him. He could move himself from one end of the room to the other,
from one conversation to the next. He was a
politician.

Couthon was part of the Jacobin faction. He
sat on the Welfare Committee, he administered
the Reign of Terror. Many of the leading Jaco-
bins, including Robespierre, died on the same
day that he did. But Couthon managed to delay
the process which, by then, had become remark-
ably streamlined. It most likely took as much as

a quarter of an hour to arrange Couthon in a reasonable position, a humane position. Making arrangements is no easy task.

✢ ✢ ✢

There is a cultural history of wheelchairs:

Clara, from the *Heidi* stories, in a high-backed, rattan wheelchair, impractical, Victorian, rickety—well-suited for being crushed beneath a jagged mountain precipice.

Professor X, from the *X-Men* comics, in a curved wheelchair made of chrome—futuristic, elegant, but just as impractical—like something sketched by the left hand of Philippe Starck.

Dr. Strangelove, from Stanley Kubrick's *Dr. Strangelove*, seated in a wheelchair that could have been borrowed from any hospital—impersonal, impractical—a stark contrast, depending on how you look at it, to the film's surroundings, the immaculately designed set by Ken Adam: *Gentlemen, you can't fight in here! This is the War Room!*

Question: Did Stanley Kubrick know what he was doing when he put Peter Sellers in a boring neutral hospital wheelchair, one as universally recognizable and unremarkable as a doorknob?

✤ ✤ ✤

Terry Eagleton *Signs which pass themselves off as natural, which offer themselves as the only conceivable way of viewing the world, are by that token authoritarian and ideological. It is one of the functions of ideology to "naturalize" social reality, to make it seem as innocent and unchangeable as Nature itself.*

If one is a wheelchair user, a wheelchair is never just a wheelchair. A wheelchair carries signs, it has a form, and it expresses a function. But if one is not a wheelchair user, is a wheelchair then just a wheelchair?

I can no longer see the category of wheelchair user from a distance. I have lost the ability to ignore distinctions, my memory cannot let go of these categorical distinctions. They are interwoven with my sensory apparatus. A child learns to speak, and in the beginning, *woof* is anything with four legs that moves on the ground, *duck* is anything with wings and a beak. Once these categories have been dissolved, they never return again. But there are many people who never learn to see anything other than *a wheelchair.*

My new Permobil had power steering and a different noise for the horn, a small, electronic *Ahem*. I didn't like using it. It was too awkward. I got good at maneuvering, the new steering made it easy. I learned not to drive over peoples' feet, especially not with the heavy back wheels. I learned to be patient. To drive slowly behind those who walked slowly, to wait for an opening.

To be a wheelchair user is to be forced upon other people. In order to move ahead on a narrow sidewalk, or through a heavy door, one must negotiate the way forward, one must push through. One must be in the way of others. The principal (of various schools) didn't want to prioritize automatic door openers: *Aren't the other students happy to help out by holding the doors open for you, isn't it a good thing for them to learn to help others?* Those who are constantly exposed to moral experiences can also be expected to offer an opportunity of moral instruction for others.

Notice of Appeal to the Office of Social Security, September 2, 1986

Our view is that our son, so far as it is possible with regard to his condition, should have the same upbringing opportunities as healthy children do.

✤ ✤ ✤

In the vacation months between elementary and middle school, I went to my first summer camp. It was a camp for those with rare diagnoses. Those of *us* with rare diagnoses. This formulation seems unnatural to me now. How could it be an *us*? My diagnosis belonged to me, I didn't belong to it. I was not a part of any such community.

I can remember several details from this camp. I remember the pre-sliced bread. I remember the slivers of brown cheese hardened at the edges. I remember the waffles and the juice; I remember the smell of the institutional kitchen, and the aftertaste that permeated all of the food.

I discovered that diagnoses create hierarchies. I, who was able to walk and to speak without drooling or stuttering, was near the top. At the pinnacle were those with illnesses that were not visible, those who might pass as normal if they strained themselves. I was not really one of those, but I was close enough, on the perimeter of the innermost circle.

Back then, I thought of them as the lucky ones. Later, I was grateful for my wheelchair, which sometimes bore my stigma for me. It became a kind of talisman, a shield. It is quite another thing to be the person who walks strangely, speaks strangely, to be the person who gives rise to discomfort.

At the same time, it was a bitter experience. I *was* one of the others, I had merely avoided realizing it up to that point. This camp *was* for children like me; in one way or another, I did belong there, I belonged in this category of children. It didn't feel right, and yet it did. I required my wheelchair to go any distance more than a hundred feet, I could not straighten my elbows out any farther than they would go.

It was a normal summer camp. We paddled in canoes. Practiced shooting with bows and arrows. It was a normal summer camp for abnormal children. The only notable aspect was that there were slightly more camp counselors.

It was anything *but* a normal summer camp. It was a gathering place, a basket of assorted wares. The only thing we had in common was something that could not be spoken aloud, neither by us nor by any of the camp counselors. They, who were also young, were there to do good. They had applied for summer jobs at this camp to make the world a better place, to bring joy into these small, sad lives. And then they had to deal with kids like me, children who had lived lives outside of institutional contexts, who didn't really understand what we were doing in a camp like this. That must have been difficult for them.

I didn't belong there. I didn't have anything to do with a place like that. I could not accept it. I went off on my own. Read books in my room. I wanted to be elsewhere. I was a preteen, and here, at camp, the counselors took great pains to make sure we had all brushed our teeth and washed ourselves.

Among his own, the stigmatized individual can use his disadvantage as a basis for organizing life, but he must resign himself to a half-world to do so.

Erving Goffman

A race was held for wheelchair users. It didn't help that everyone's wheelchair had the same capped speed limit of ten kilometers an hour, as designated by the Road Traffic Act and regulated by the technicians of the Mobility Aid Centre. I still won. I was better at steering. In other words, I had the best fine motor skills. If this was a competition, it was between the diagnoses.

I brought my books and games with me to the summer camp. I had discovered Magic: The Gathering. It was a card game that was a blend of strategy and fantasy, dragons, demons, and attack formations. It reminded me of role-playing games, only you weren't allowed to collaborate with others. It was about winning.

The game was quickly outlawed at camp. It was exclusionary. It was too complicated for everyone to participate; the children with learning disabilities didn't meet the preconditions for play and, therefore, no one was allowed to play.

Then I met Cecilie. I don't remember what her diagnosis was, but it was of the non-visible sort; she was in the innermost circle. Compared to the others, there wasn't that much wrong with her, or me, and that may be how we thought about it—that we were almost normal.

My first experiences of being physically superior were the result of that summer. To be stronger than someone else, faster, more precise in my movements. I saw vulnerability from the outside for the first time. It didn't make me nicer or more empathetic, but it did whet my appetite.

We danced together at camp, Cecilie and I. We were not allowed to be alone in our rooms so late in the evenings, that was the time for sleeping. A girl with Down syndrome was convinced we were a couple, the way a little sister might have been. We couldn't shut the door. It was against the rules to lock anyone out, to exclude anyone.

Cecilie was small and thin, like me. I remember her arms, her nearly flat chest. We were able to walk, both of us, she farther than me. Indoors, we walked side by side. Down by the water, I drove my wheelchair while she walked beside me. It was better for me when she walked on my left side. Then I could hold her hand. I needed my right hand to steer. We walked along the water before bedtime. We stood at the window, with its thin, dusty institutional curtains. I had on a heavy black T-shirt, with an embossed pattern, that I took off. I wasn't ashamed of my body, not there. It was almost like taking off your clothes at the hospital, and I had done that on many occasions.

Then it was over. We were in Oslo again; Cecilie lived only one subway stop away. But now we were back in the real world. I didn't want to be her boyfriend there, in the real world, I didn't even want to be her friend. I felt ashamed about this for a long time, and then, at some point, it merely made me sad to think of it. I didn't want to be her boyfriend because all of my friends were normal. I could be normal too, almost, as long as I was the only one like me.

Erving Goffman *The self must not only be offered, it must be accepted.*

At summer camp, everything was clear. Everything was accessible to the adult gaze. The doors had no thresholds. All of the furniture had wheels that could be pushed in and out of the room. The curtains were sheer, with ugly geometrical patterns. The sun rose and everyone woke up too early.

The camp was not for young people, it wasn't for people at all, it was for patients, for users. It was well-intentioned, well-regulated, an expression of well-being and care. It was located permanently in the shadow of that other life, a haunting possibility of a state of emergency. It was, in the words of Giorgio Agamben, what opens up *when the state of exception begins to become the rule.*

I never went back. But I did hold on to a single good memory, the memory of dancing with Cecilie. A dance floor had been rigged up in the cafeteria. Cecilie and I danced, slowly, I on my unsteady legs. Just there, on the dance floor, in the midst of the other children and teenagers, those who wobbled and drooled and stammered, a small space opened up, for a little while. We wobbled there, in our own space, a space in which my experiences were the only thing that mattered, mine and Cecilie's. Our bodies touched, and she and I swayed together, this was an experience that didn't belong to anything else, it constituted its own place, its own time. It was my most poignant memory of *kairos* up until that point, the feeling of a gap opening up in time, until, just afterward, when we walked along the lake, I asked her if she would be my girlfriend.

Places of this kind are outside of all places, even though it may be possible to indicate their location in reality. Because these places are absolutely different from all the sites that they reflect and speak about, I shall call them, by way of contrast to utopias, heterotopias.

Michel Foucault

Dance is magical. It is a private act in a public space; it is a secret that takes place in the open. I am not a good dancer—*good* is not a relevant word, I can hardly move to a beat without falling down. I danced a few times in high school, and I fell down a few times.

It's summer in Bordeaux, and Ida's cousin is getting married. We are newly in love and have flown there because we are able to do such things, to order plane tickets to France and pick up and go, go attend a wedding. At Charles de Gaulle, the airport personnel try carrying me, and drop me on the ground; it takes half an hour for someone to unlock the only wheelchair-accessible bathroom at the airport. In the tiny country village, Ida has to push me around in a manual wheelchair, as the day grows hotter and we each grow more and more irritable. These are all details. We get lost on the way back to the airport, we are eaten up by the insects that hover around the small river next our hotel. All of this is immaterial, because on the eve of the wedding, we dance together on a wooden platform under the open sky. "I never thought we'd be able to do something like this," Ida says, and I never thought we'd be able to do something like this either. And yet, there we are, beneath a starry sky, and three years later, almost to the day, we dance at our own wedding, I don't fall down, we hold on to each other.

It could have been different. I could have lived a different life.

I went to a run-of-the-mill primary school, a run-of-the-mill middle school, I applied to the high school of my choice, the one that required the best grades for admission, and I was accepted on my own merits. None of this was a given. The work I put into it was necessary, but it might not have been sufficient. Twenty years earlier, or even ten years earlier, things might have been different. Fifty years earlier, things almost certainly would have been different. I would have been sent to a different school, given a *special* education, or perhaps not even have been given the chance for an education at all. The world I would have inhabited would have been a smaller world, a world that would remain shut. But this is not what happened. One circle opened up to another circle. The horizon expanded.

In my final year of high school, I got my driver's license. I put in well over a hundred practice hours, I practice-drove constantly for six months. This was necessary for me to master a steering system that didn't involve my legs. While my left hand rested on a lever that controlled the gas and brakes, my right maneuvered a miniature steering wheel that was six inches in diameter and offered zero resistance. Minuscule nudges meant the difference between twenty-five and fifty miles per hour, the difference between the road and the ditch.

Learning this took an incredible amount of time. But without a driver's license, I would not be able to attend the folk high school in Denmark, which was set in a remote location. I wanted to go abroad. I had set my mind on this particular school, which focused solely on film, and I wasn't about to give up. They had their own film studio, four editing rooms, a sound studio, and two cinemas. I liked film. I had to go to this folk high school. It was that simple, it was that difficult. This was the work I had to put into it.

Many factors shore up a privilege such as this, to be able to attend whichever school one desires, to be able to do whatever work is required to get there. I was not as aware of my social advantages back then—the fact that I enjoyed freedoms that others did not have, the freedom to believe that my dreams could come true.

This did not mean, however, that I didn't have to work for it. I put in the many hours it took me to earn my license, my parents made sure I had a vehicle in which I could practice, which meant they had to apply for the resources, procure the car, and then have it reconstructed to suit me, not to mention the endless hours we put in practice driving together, my father and I, to supplement the hours spent with the driving instructor. It was hard work; we did it together.

At the beginning, I drove at an extremely slow speed; one tiny twitch, and the car would lurch uncontrollably ahead. Learning to drive was a labor of patience. I was already at one with the wheelchair and had thus believed it would be easy to drive a car, but that's not how it works, nothing having to do with the body comes easily to me. I am able to read quickly, think quickly, learn quickly. But my body has its own, slower pace. I cannot hurry. I often require help.

From the time I was in my early teens, I began to share the work with my parents, the work of *being myself in the world*, outside my family, and little by little, I became aware of the others, those who didn't have anyone to help them with this work. Those who never attended a normal high school, who never completed high school, who never traveled abroad. These people existed too. I met some of them once at summer camp, and then I never saw them again.

There exists an apparatus intended to provide support. It is a heavy device and hard to operate. It is analog and steam-powered, with unlabeled levers and gears that have rusted in place. It is the social apparatus, and it is located in the basement, down a flight of stairs and behind a door, and the door is locked and the key has been misplaced.

This apparatus is geared toward another world, another future. It is this future I have glimpsed from the corner of one eye, and from which I have fled. All of the work I have done has been for the purpose of avoiding this particular life, which cannot be acknowledged as life. Which is a surrogate, a replacement.

Improvement of the condition should not be expected, it will most likely get worse, and it is therefore of utmost importance that circumstances are optimally arranged so as to allow him to lead as normal a life as possible with his family and in society. He has very good capabilities.

Doctor's note, September 21, 1988

Nothing that happened afterward was a given. Higher education, job, family. From a statistical perspective, these were far from certain. My *very good capabilities* helped somewhat. What helped even more was to have a family who had mastered the Norwegian Social Services system, who mastered the world to which I would have access.

Work helped; work is necessary to keep this world afloat. But work alone is never sufficient.

During the first year pursuing my master's degree, I began to teach at the University of Oslo. It was nerve-racking to be responsible for leading a course while still a student myself. I later learned that this was not necessarily a rite of passage; in fact, it was rather unusual, a sign that there were other opportunities, alternatives.

I was aware these other opportunities existed. My parents are academics, my friends applied to the same places as me. I'd always had high expectations. And yet, I was afraid of looking down. There is a duality in this. In the papers that I have stacked on shelves in my office, I am still a child with a diagnosis, a vulnerable child. I am still a child who will require Social Services assistance for my whole life. And it's true: I cannot walk up the stairs without another person supporting me; I cannot lift the heaviest of the cast-iron pots off its shelf.

For a brief period, American universities advertised academic positions like mine with the proviso that the candidate must be able to lift thirty-five pounds. My own limit is somewhere between eight and twelve pounds, which is slightly more than the weight of a newborn baby. I know well why this requirement was included in American job advertisements, and that such requirements were eventually found to be illegal, but there will always be other avenues to the unexpressed goal, which is to keep those like me out.

It's possible for opposing truths to live side by side. I am privileged and vulnerable, I have worked hard and require assistance, I have arrived where I am by my own efforts, primarily because I live in a society that recognizes such efforts and supplements them when needed. Social Services does not understand this, does not wish to understand. It is as though I've defied the law of gravity. Social Services asks if my wife can't take on the larger portion of household chores. It asks why I am requesting more assistance, is it because my health is in danger, is it because I'm unable to fulfill my role as a father, is my son's health in danger?

Social Services poses a hundred tiny demands as to how I should formulate my needs, how, precisely, my wretchedness should be described. It would like me to pretend, because it refuses to realize the truth—that I am happy, that I am doing fine *and I need help*. Social Services casts me a knowing wink, it asks whether I am truly okay, okay enough to leave Social Services alone, to let it turn its mild face rather toward those who are content to remain wretched.

It is a paradox whenever one of the wretched succeeds in the world, travels abroad, receives a Ph.D. fellowship, becomes a university professor. This success belongs to the exceptions, it must, for if such paradoxes were to become the norm, if Social Services would earnestly succeed in its mission, who knows what might happen? Maybe everyone in need would start requesting services.

There are others like me. I have eventually come to know them, but it's taken fifteen years, we have each followed our own paths through the woods, usually without so much as a glimpse of one another, and it's only now that we are starting to emerge, that we can nod to one another in acknowledgment: *Oh? So, you made it too?*

But we are tired. I am tired. The work is endless, which doesn't help. Onward and upward.

The stigmatized individual can also attempt to correct his condition indirectly by devoting much private effort to the mastery of areas of activity ordinarily felt to be closed on incidental and physical grounds to one with his shortcoming.

Erving
Goffman

Stigma is *spoiled identity*, Goffman writes, a sense of one's self that is tainted or broken, damaged or rotten, and the damage is like an infected wound, it threatens to spread the rot to all the other parts. When this happens, it's tempting to try saving parts of one's self *from* one's self, to say to one's self that *this* part of me doesn't have anything to do with *that* part, and that *this* part, which is healthy and sound, isn't related to *that* part, which is sick, broken, rotten.

This is not what I want. I wish to accept myself, my whole self. I have almost managed to do it. Unfortunately, the same cannot be said about the world.

There is such a thing as an unlived life, and even if it is nothing but air bubbles in water, a shadow of something that does not exist, I am nevertheless able to see small flashes of it, it dances around me and every now and then becomes recognizable. I associate it with certain times, certain places.

I've stolen a thought from *Anna Karenina*: all wheelchair-accessible cities are alike; each inaccessible city is inaccessible in its own way. There are places in my consciousness that are patrolled by Terminus; there are places where I have drawn up the barriers myself.

In the summer of 2002, I sat in the second story of a house in St. Petersburg, sensing my helplessness. The morning turned into late morning and then afternoon. Around one p.m., I grew impatient, and when the clock rolled around to three p.m., I began to feel desperate.

I was waiting for my study peers, I couldn't get ahold of them. Their cell phones were turned off or the batteries had died.

It was Saturday. I looked out the window. The area in front of the building was empty. The ground was dusty. There were some scraggly weeds, the overall impression was one of neglect, like most things in Russia, Russia as I remember it from those days. Cars with trunks buckled open, tied down with rope. Elevators with half the buttons missing on their panels. Half-finished skyscrapers, roads petering out to nothing.

It was strange to feel abandoned in this manner, I wasn't used to it. I was used to living in Oslo, where many parts of the city were admittedly inaccessible to me just as they were here, of course, with the difference being that I knew which parts these were. Half of the trams, all of the buses, perhaps two-thirds of the shops, restaurants, and cafés, it's hard to give a precise estimate. I was used to navigating according to my own map, with my own starting point. I already knew that the world offered a limited number of alternatives, that

I had to think carefully about where I would go to study abroad because I would first have to think about where it would be *possible* for me to study. But I was good at making plans, I could see a path forward.

I also believed, even though I was not totally clear about it, that there weren't any real external limitations to what I could do, to the kind of life I could live. One logical consequence of this belief was the further belief that it all boiled down to myself, and that I was limited only by my own qualities—talent, motivation, capabilities. There were plenty of narratives to reinforce such a belief fifteen years ago; there are even more such narratives today. These stories harmonize beautifully with a political economy in which people are either contributors or expenditures. They are stories well suited to a culture in which the body is more a prop, a source of shame or pride, than a setting and parameter for a life.

The image of myself alone in a room in Russia, unable to go anywhere, has assumed a certain value, an intensity, even if I don't quite know why. Perhaps it's because I know that I will never return *there*, even if I know that, sooner or later, I will once again find myself helpless in a room somewhere else. But it is also because Russia has taken on a symbolic dimension for me—almost everyone who visits Russia, if even on a screen or through a book, ends up writing it into their own personal mythology—as an antipode to California, as the heavy and unchanging element of *opposition* in the world. Russia is the stone on which the teeth clamp down.

Nevertheless, throughout its first century, St. Petersburg was a city of pilings and planks; its czar had to erect the city in the middle of an enormous, mosquito-infested marsh, a task that required determination and violence. After Peter the Great, a city stood where none had stood before, but it was only after the German-born empress Catherine that it became a European capital with palaces and avenues and vistas. A city of canals modeled on Amsterdam but, according to classic Russian reasoning, scaled to an empire, not to a human scale. And all of it built of stone. That's how one may become "the Great": by building something new, or by building it with stone.

I dabbled in a romance with Russia that lasted from the middle of my teens to the middle of my twenties, a masochistic romance, since Russia was so uninterested and aloof that the effect was rather sadistic. In Russia, I received clear, frequent remarks of the sort that were rarely or never said out loud at home in Norway.

What are you doing here?
There's no place for you here.
Go away.

Russia has never hesitated to say such words aloud, and wheelchair users are far down the list of groups that have been subjected to these words throughout history. But we are there, on the list, in proud fellowship.

Fyodor Tyutchev *Russia cannot be grasped with the mind . . . One can only believe in Russia.*

In other words, it is a land where ideas meet materiality with disdain. But it was this materiality that *I* met, as much in the hostile faces as in the wide streets that could only be crossed by descending stairs down to the pedestrian passageways.

What are you doing here?
There's no place for you here.
Go away.

It does something to you to hear these words so clearly, from overhead, repeatedly. The Russian intelligentsia has always been torn between resistance and subordination, and the dream of the good czar is still alive. It is the abused child's rationale of their parents' behavior—the problem must be *me*, they can't possibly be doing this because *they* are bad . . . *I must try harder to be likable.*

In those days, I was occupied with viewing myself, viewing my life, in the light of something grander. I wanted above all else to achieve a philosophical or ideological platform, and I wanted this platform to provide me with a sense of meaning. As I've grown older, this need has vanished. It strikes me increasingly as a need to escape my body and all that it is unable to do on its own. The search for a higher purpose can also be an attempt to flee.

In Russia, I was more dependent on help from others than in any other country I've visited. The result is that these journeys have become very valuable to me. It's valuable to recognize those things that we take for granted in one's own country. It is also valuable to recognize which features of one's own country are amplified or diminished in other places. History does not move uniformly; different forces are at play, pulling in multiple directions.

I was sitting on the second floor of the Norwegian University Centre in St. Petersburg when I said to myself: *Enough.* There had been several occasions when I could have said *Enough,* but I had neither recognized nor acknowledged them. They had been invisible, or unacceptable, because I carried such a strong and yet also vague notion about what success should look like for me, about what it meant to be good enough. This notion of mine was based on being like everyone else, only better—smarter and more disciplined, more hardworking, less forgiving. Such a stance seemed worthwhile and necessary because it gave me the motivation to propel myself onward, always onward, and maybe it was precisely because of this impetus to prove myself worthy that I never stopped to ask where it was leading, or in which direction I was headed.

It's hard to say *Enough* out loud when you have been living under a weight for so long, when you've been running on adrenaline for many years. But it's good to say it, to say to yourself, I don't *have* to do this, I don't have to try to push in where there's no way in, to try carving out a space where there is none.

In Russia I was forced to acknowledge certain limitations. After the introductory courses came the courses for my major. This entailed a three-month-long stay in St. Petersburg, and it dawned on me that I was not willing to take on the required effort—because the only reward awaiting me was more of the same effort. This place, this country, would never have anything to offer me other than a hard time.

Saying *Enough* was about accepting the world as it was, and releasing the dream about another world, and for this reason it was painful, just as all experiences of loss are painful. Grief accompanies all such experiences, grief over what is no longer possible, and what can no longer become a reality. Grief is the recognition that something, or someone, is gone forever; this *someone* can also be a self, or a version of a self.

Erving Goffman   *The self must not only be offered, it must be accepted.*

In Russia, I began to recognize that other limitations were more important than the one dividing the possible from the impossible. There was a boundary between what merited a lifetime of toil and what did not. I didn't know *the life trajectory of either possibility*, what was on the one side or the other, but merely experiencing the impact of these alternatives meant that I began, slowly, to seek out places where I was welcome, accepted. This was a beginning, of sorts.

❖ ❖ ❖

The stigmatized individual can also attempt to correct his condition indirectly by devoting much private effort to the mastery of areas of activity ordinarily felt to be closed on incidental and physical grounds to one with his shortcoming.

Erving
Goffman

Change, if it is fundamental and emotionally profound, does not occur without resistance. I was in St. Petersburg for one month; I studied in Amsterdam for half a year. Both were bad places to study, for not only were both made up of streets interrupted by canals, they were both *historical* and *picturesque*, which is another way of saying *old-fashioned* and *impractical*. At least one car per month regularly drives into a canal in Amsterdam. These cars have to be fished out again by the same companies that used to fish panicked horses out of the cold, murky waters.

The old saying goes that *insanity is doing the same thing over and over again and expecting different results each time.* Which different result had I expected? That my surroundings would up and change themselves? I once wrote a short story in which

I depicted Amsterdam as a labyrinth, and this is what I think of still whenever I picture the city, as a place in which to get lost.

I visited again with some friends the year after I'd studied there. One evening, they returned home later than I did, they had lost their sense of direction at the center of the labyrinth, at a university building from which the spiraling concentric streets begin spreading outward. It's unwalkable, the geography curls inward there, land turns to water, solid ground disappears.

Along the bicycle lanes that follow Amsterdam's canals, I was able to move quickly in my wheelchair, but the *historical, picturesque* houses all had long, narrow, steep stairways up to the entries. Why was it I chose to study *there*, exactly, why did I go to *that* city? Even now I don't have a good answer, other than that I enjoyed banging my head against a wall, steadfast in the belief that the wall would eventually give way.

The university buildings were accessible. University buildings are often the most open, most accessible buildings, they are the public arenas to which it is easiest to gain access. Private homes are a different story, as are underground clubs, bars, hideouts.

I studied in Amsterdam for half a year, remaining all the time on the surface of things, never finding what I was looking for. I took classes on the philosophy of consciousness, on the relationship between programming language and human language, on formal semantics and pragmatics. This is the knowledge that can lead to the development of artificial intelligence, and to the understanding of why AI is something very different from consciousness, so that, perhaps, we will be able to put a finger on what it is that separates explanation and comprehension.

I am able to *explain* why I went to Amsterdam, which had to do with the size of the city, the topics of study available there, but, most important, it had to do with the expectation that studying abroad was an obligatory step for ambitious, academically superior students. And yet I find it difficult, even if I try hard, to comprehend what I was doing there.

The explanation is both complicated and frightfully simple. It was an attempt to fumble my way forward on my life's project, to put it abstractly. It was my attempt to *do what you do*, and *what you do*, if you have a background like mine, in my situation, is to study abroad for a period of time. At Sciences Po, Oxford, Harvard, or, if necessary, another well-known American or European university. This is how one may demonstrate one's belonging, one's ability to maintain certain standards, one's status as a world mover and shaker. So, that's what I did. It required more hours of hard work, more effort, than I could have anticipated, but I continued banging my head against the wall until the wall finally gave way. On the inside was another wall. This is how labyrinths are built, after all.

In the first month, when there was sunshine, I lived in an empty building. It was a student residence on the Prinsengracht, *the canal of the prince*, in the most picturesque part of the historic town center. The cafés, which I could not enter, had tables down near the canals, I was sometimes brave enough to order a cup of coffee. The student residence was the only wheelchair-accessible dormitory the university had to offer, and it was slated to be renovated. The foyer was large and dark, sometimes there were construction crews inside fiddling with things, they sent me bewildered glances, as if I was a remnant from another phase of the institution's life.

I cooked premade ravioli or tortellini on one of the two hot plates and stirred in premade red pesto, I sometimes made a salad too. The dorm room had large windows facing an inner courtyard filled with trees and plants; I thought of botanical gardens, zoological gardens.

I rode past the Anne Frank House and the church nearby every day. The church bells would ring every fifteen minutes. I listened to Michelle Shocked, *The Texas Campfire Tapes*, "5 a.m. in Amsterdam":

It's 5 a.m. in Amsterdam
And this is how I know
There's a church beside a park

And it fills the dying dark
With five strokes
There it is again

I know of no song that better suits a city than that one; it still makes me feel romantic. Fifteen years have passed since I was there, and revisiting those lyrics is all nostalgia requires. I was never as lonely as I was in those autumn days, and yet even that period has a tonality, an echo I need to hear again from time to time.

I once read about a Russian woman who had lived through terror, through the Stalin years. In a brief period, she had lost more than most people lose over the course of their entire lives, and she did not seem the least bit sentimental when she said, *But remember, that was my youth.*

From the start of October it rained nonstop. In November I realized that I was depressed. Maybe the rain helped me to realize it more quickly than I otherwise would; maybe it took longer because I had something external that I could blame.

I was able to arrange an hour with a Dutch psychologist, we communicated in English, neither of us was comfortable doing so. I was unable to explain why I felt down, and he was unable to understand why I was in the Netherlands. He asked me some awkward questions about the wheelchair and whether I experienced life as difficult. One hour was enough. He was trying, I think, to uncover an external cause that still belonged to *me*, to this strange student who had looked him up.

Later that fall, still in Amsterdam, I admitted to myself that I didn't have a girlfriend, and that I wanted one. I admitted that I wanted to be a father one day, and that there was no way of knowing whether that would ever happen. Most of my twenties were behind me by the time I could put such thoughts into words. It was like finally recognizing a face I had been seeing in dreams for years.

A form of clarity followed these admissions to myself. I decided to go home. It wasn't long until Christmas. My parents came down to help me move back. We took the ferry from Kiel. I had planned to stay in Amsterdam for the whole year, until the summer. But I couldn't do it. It was a defeat and it was a victory. I felt the feeling of freedom that comes from canceling plans, not living up to expectations, of instead choosing to do what is truly necessary.

The most difficult task before going home was to talk with the study counselor who had arranged a place for me to live and who had been informed that I hadn't signed up for my spring courses. He sent me an email that was intermittently sharp and angry, as if I was a close relative who had behaved badly. We spoke briefly by phone, and his tone was the same. All of that effort from him, and I couldn't manage to stay the course?

After I moved back to Norway, I found a psychologist I could speak with in my own language, and it took a few hours, or maybe only ten minutes, before I was able to say out loud exactly why I was unhappy. *I want the same thing as everyone else. But I'm not like everyone else. It's harder for me to get what I want.*

I told him about *Wings of Desire* and why the fate of the angel had moved me so deeply. As I said this, I understood the obvious therapeutic metaphor I was offering him.

It all happened so fast, I was surprised. I had thought that therapy was about tentatively seeking answers over the course of many years. I had expected long psychoanalytic work, digging down through tightly packed layers of history in order to understand myself. But I had already done this work. The insight was already so close to the surface that I could see its contours. I had been working through these thoughts for several years, I had simply neglected to acknowledge to myself that I was doing so.

Maybe it was because the insights were so terribly obvious, as the psychologist pointed out. He said: *A lot of this is already known to those who know you.* He gave me permission to say out loud what I knew, and to believe that I was not the only person who knew it.

It isn't my fault that my body is the way it is; it isn't anyone's fault. It's no secret that my body is the way it is. And, most important: I'm allowed to feel sad that this is so.

In fiction, physical dexterity can be traded for mental ability, body can be sacrificed for mind. Odin gave an eye for a gulp of wisdom. Professor X from *X-Men* had to be paralyzed in order to acquire his telepathic abilities. I've met people who believe I've made a similar decision, either before or after my birth. They would like for a cathedral of meaning to loom over all of it, that every life should be formed by an inner, moral logic.

This attitude does not necessarily have to be religious, it doesn't have to be dogmatic—an insistence that everything happens according to a divine plan. It can just as well be some banality that bubbles up in the form of sayings.

Every cloud has a silver lining . . . When one door closes, another one opens. Whatever doesn't kill you, makes you stronger.

Such moral logic makes it easier to talk about a person's life and trajectory as though it were both predestined and intrinsically meaningful. It is a narrative template that allows the storyteller to cut out everything superfluous. I am an author and academic because I am a wheelchair user. I am suited for a wheelchair because I'm an intellectual. Which of these conclusions leads to the best story?

There's no space for the world in a story. To tell a story is to remember, and to remember is to forget.

Jorge Luis Borges wrote a fable about a man by the name of Funes. He falls from his horse and wakes up paralyzed, but with a perfect memory. Funes lies, not moving, in his bed, recalling *everything* —even beyond the photographic, which also has its own blurriness, its blind spots. Funes sees the world as it actually is.

This new ability proves catastrophic for Funes. His memory is overwhelming. He's unable to create a system and drowns in the details. A dog seen from the front is not the same dog as seen from the side, for the memories differ. He cannot put the two pictures together, to think of them as *the same dog*. The world is too detailed. Unable to think abstractly, stuck in the concrete, his thoughts become paralyzed as well. He is unable to move in his thoughts, for to think is to forget.

This book has been written and rewritten multiple times. For each episode and memory I call forth, I am writing something away. I retrieve it from within myself and place it on the table. I contemplate it. Does it fit into the whole? Does it fit into the story I want to have about myself? Am I letting slip some information that I don't want to let slip? When I was eight years old, I shoved one of the girls in my class, or I knocked something off her desk. The teacher asked me to apologize, and I said: *If what I did was wrong, then I apologize.*

I can still sense part of myself in those old papers, in spite of everything. I am familiar with clinical language, academic language, with all kinds of formal language. My personality has a strong analytical bent, even when I'm in the middle of an argument with Ida, I hear this little voice that says: *What happens if you say this, and not that?* I have had to learn to dial down my tendency to self-censor because it's better to be furious in the moment than to try to back out and set oneself up as the judge.

The clinical gaze awaits me in the mirror, in every reflective surface. I see what is noteworthy about my body, what a clinician would take note of. I see the spindly legs and the overdimensioned shoes holding the twisted feet in place, I see the arms bent at a particular angle. But I also see that this is *me*.

The clinical gaze will follow me all my life. I can attempt to face it with my writing, to write it into submission, but I cannot write it away. I can become more familiar with it, I can try to understand the beast and its function, but I cannot think it away any more than I can think away my own life story.

Sometimes I fantasize about being done. About having reached a point where I have fixed every practical problem, answered every question, finished everything that needs to be finished, put my work away. And then I remember that this is a fantasy about death, it has nothing whatsoever to do with human life. Onward and upward.

Gradually, as in a geological process, time is compressed and converted into place. I've traveled from Norway to California six times—in 2005, 2008, 2009, 2011, 2013, and 2014—via Paris, via Amsterdam, via London. California is the same place, with the same sensory memories attached to it. The scent of eucalyptus, the intense sunshine, and the surprisingly crisp air, when are these memories from, from which of the years?

In the midst of these travels, Ida becomes enmeshed in the memories. I am still able to recall

California without her, but I have to work at it. I work, I remember my work, and I work at remembering my work. This is my life now, together with Ida, the life I always wanted to live. With my family, in my home, at my job.

And you may ask yourself, Well . . . how did I get here?   **Talking Heads**

In 2005, the first time I went to California, a group of us traveled to visit other friends who were studying there. They were living in the second story of a little house behind a tall gate, with the same kind of elaborate, overcrowded garden that can be found everywhere on the outskirts of Berkeley. I fell asleep late on the first night, woke up groggy and in the wrong time zone. The gurgle of the toilet was a strangely foreign sound, and it felt foreign to sleep in someone else's house. When I was younger, I rarely had sleepovers with friends, it was impractical to sleep on a mattress on the floor and shower in someone else's slippery bathtub. To spend the night somewhere else still felt exotic to me, an entire journey in and of itself. These two, friends of mine from Norway, had brought with them the feeling of *home*, now they were living here in California, and I saw what was possible.

The next day, we walked to the university. It took almost an hour to walk there; the distances invited one to drive, but we wanted to see the surroundings. The neighborhoods reminded me somewhat of the stretches of old villas in Oslo neighborhoods, Vinderen, Tåsen, and Nordberg, but the gardens here were full of cactuses and exotic flowers, and small Spanish-style haciendas sat alongside functionalist houses and imitation log cabins. The sidewalks were made of concrete slabs, and my manual wheelchair lurched over all the bumps that tree roots had pushed up.

There were trees absolutely everywhere, palms and pines, and the scent of eucalyptus. I fell in love with Berkeley on that trip, instinctively and bodily, through its aromas and tastes. Jet lag only heightened the intoxication; I woke at four in the morning and was famished; by nine in the evening, I was overwhelmed by impressions.

We drove around San Francisco, up and down the nearly vertical hills, out over the Golden Gate to Marin County to the north, to Muir Woods, where the redwood trees tower like memorials to the dawn of time. We walked the streets in the Mission, on the southeast end, drank Bloody Marys with chipotle in the Castro. All the time I kept a sharp lookout for details, as if I was planning to break out of Alcatraz, but it was in that I wanted, not out, I wanted to know if there could be a place for me here, on my own.

The elevators at the BART stations were quite large, but some of them had two doors that stood at ninety-degree angles to each other. I tried sizing up the situation, I thought and evaluated. If you rolled through the one door in an electric wheelchair with a large turning radius, would it be possible to get out through the other door? Many of the student residences were new, but the international student residence was in a hundred-year-old building. How did things work here? Who made the decisions? Who did I have to write to, to speak with? What had to happen? It's always about the details; when I am sufficiently nervous, whenever I *want* something enough, my thoughts branch out like ice crystals, I try to think through every possibility at once. It's a feverish feeling, these imperatives keep me awake at night.

We were there for a week. We went to a concert at Boom Boom Room. Drove out to Point Reyes to look for whales; we didn't see anything but the sunset over the Pacific, but that was more than enough. We ate burgers at Sand Dollar Restaurant in Stinson Beach. It was November, some of the days felt the way June does in Norway, with the wind slightly cooler, the sun slightly stronger. More than anything else, I felt I wanted to live there.

One afternoon my father called. It must have been evening already in Norway. I thought something must be wrong. I was right, partly. The diagnosis that had been given when I was three—*that* was wrong. The results from a new and more precise genetic examination had arrived: I had tested negative for the marker that went along with the previous diagnosis. It was as simple as that.

Since an early age, I had known that I had spinal muscular atrophy. It was never a definitive statement about who I was, but I thought about my diagnosis the way I thought about the color of my eyes or how many fingers I had. And now suddenly it was gone, a puff of smoke.

It was not a long phone call. The connection was bad, and the international fees were expensive. For a few minutes after hanging up, I sat completely still, unable to move. I could see myself sitting there, I wondered how long it would take before I started to cry. And then it happened.

I sobbed uncontrollably, more than I ever remembered having cried before. It was like a deluge, like moorings had suddenly snapped. The grief welled up and splashed out. I was an inordinate distance from home, and in a strange, unexpected way I had been set free.

A diagnosis is intimate. It is a conclusion. If it is given after years of uncertainty, it can seem liberating. It affirms that all the worries were not unnecessary, that there *was*, in fact, something wrong; it proves that your own perception of reality is the right one and that you can be trusted. It can put one at ease.

If a diagnosis describes a progressive condition, it can also be a source of unease. It conjures images of the future. It is a road map to a place you don't want to visit.

A diagnosis has its own gravitational field. It can shape identity, like other weighty concepts—gender, sexual orientation. One who has never been diagnosed is free without knowing it.

What happens when a diagnosis vanishes suddenly? Something is gone, but it was never there, and that which remains is the same as before.

Everything was as it always had been, only now it lacked a clinically precise name, and this changed everything. My body was the same, but in a changed way, it was now *mine*. And I felt a new sense of responsibility for it.

No longer did a sudden deterioration wait for me around some corner. Spinal muscular atrophy is a progressive illness, but I had not progressed. I was stronger than I should have been. I could still walk. Now I could depend on my body. It was the diagnosis that was wrong.

Although the diagnosis was gone, my body remained the same. Walking down the stairs and out into the garden is just as difficult for me as it has always been. Perhaps I have more time than I previously thought. I will still die someday. Until that day, I will still be weaker than most people I meet.

I had always outperformed the expected prognoses. Arvid, a family friend who is a geneticist, tended to say I had *Jan Grue's disease*. This I have tried to remember.

What it means is that the field of genetics is developing rapidly, but the time lines of science are not in step with everyday human life. Knowledge can change in a millisecond, but it can take decades for clinical trials to start. The discovery of antibiotics changed everything, and yet here we are now, generations later, watching as resistant bacteria morph into ever-evolving strains.

I think of the Buddhist monk in the parable, the one who refuses to label single events as lucky or unlucky, who ever only says: *We'll see.* My diagnosis was gone, and what remained was the freedom to be able to say about the future: *We'll see.*

OSL to SFO, spring 2008. I was hurtling down the runway. The airplane lurched, everything was in motion. The folded-up tray rattled in the seat back in front of me. Any minute, I would lift off, any minute now.

Two years earlier, I had finished my master's degree. Course set, back away from the gate.

One year earlier, I had become a Ph.D. candidate . . . Out onto the runway, motors revving.

Half a year earlier, I received a Fulbright scholarship to travel to UC Berkeley in California. Faster now, picking up speed. I had never had such a strong sense of being in motion, in flight. It was even stronger because I was a person who was used to sitting still, to moving slowly.

Then: the motor sputtered, threatening to lock up completely.

In the spring of 2008, I exchanged somewhere between two and three hundred emails with people in California I didn't know. To some of them I still owe a debt of gratitude, and others I still remember with vague irritation, a kind of loathing.

These emails comprise an archive of a sort distinct from the papers from my childhood. Nevertheless, they are linked by their underlying pessimism, their frugality. It's so trivial, the things we argue about. Should we spend our lives fighting about an aid device, over whether to provide wheelchair access to a student residence?

Yes, apparently, we should. I want something, and I cannot get it without a fight. I should know this by now.

That was ten years ago, and in those emails, I see a version of myself that is more vulnerable and defensive than I am now, one who *wants* so very much, for whom everything is at stake. The door that leads into *something* was wide open in those days, I knew it, but not what that something was, I could sense it, smell it, almost feel it, my entire body knew that something was there, almost within reach, without knowing what it was, but my body searched for it, I searched for it.

It is a literary sense of logic that structures this archive, because I know what California has become for me. I like to believe that I knew what it would become even in those early days. This is a retroactive construction; it could have been different. I know this too.

In a novella titled *The Garden of Forking Paths*, Borges speculates that alternate futures and alternate pasts can flow from the same moment. That is what it feels like to be entrapped by the suggestions and implications of institutional texts: the labyrinth is comprised of winding corridors, and there are multiple ways into and out of the center.

In the spring and summer of 2008, I lived with a quivering sensation in my body that would not let me relax, it hardly let me sleep at night. It was the thought of doing something that seemed unthinkable, something that seemed impractical to achieve, and therefore more worthy of pursuit, namely that I should live for a year in California, I, with my wheelchair, I, with all of my *special needs*, I, as in: myself.

The problem was finding a place to live. I had been accepted at the university, I had a fellowship, all the other kinds of formalities were in place. I had sorted out everything that needed sorting out with the welfare office's international section, including permission to export my wheelchair, which was and is the property of the Norwegian State. But the impossible thing was finding a place to live.

I couldn't believe I might be stymied by this basic obstacle. As a Fulbright Scholar and a *visiting student researcher*, I reached out to UC Berkeley's International Office one year prior to traveling to California. They didn't know anything about wheelchairs. The department managing accessible student residences, apparently unable to assist visiting foreigners, directed me back to the International Office. I belonged in two irreconcilable categories. I was an odd creature, a heretofore unknown hybrid.

The university was world famous for its accessibility. In 1964, it was the birthplace of one of the first protests of its kind when the student Ed Roberts fought for the right to live on campus instead of at the hospital where the university had sent him for lodging. I knew about all of this. It was one of the reasons why I had applied.

As a Fulbright scholar I had been promised, and then denied, a place of residence. When I reread the correspondence, the first thing that surprises me is the cold, businesslike tone I used. My memories of my emotions are much stronger than how I expressed them:

. . . there may have been a slight misunderstanding . . . I hope you'll be able to look into . . . very best regards . . .

Email to the student residence office, March 22, 2008

But then, that is the tone I always use. This is how you address institutions, those who hold the power. You give away nothing of yourself. You don't let them see any more of your vulnerabilities than you must. You say, in the politest phrases you can muster, full of modal auxiliary verbs: *Don't hit me.*

And then the institution replies:

. . . I am so sorry that we are not able to . . . I have made some inquiries for you . . .

Reply from the student residence office, March 24

The temperature increases by notches as the spring progresses. It's not looking good, and the time has to be now. The Fulbright scholarship was granted for *this* year, not for any other year. My tone in the emails is still businesslike, only slightly more desperate, while the institution remains imperturbably dismissive:

From the university, June 5

. . . unfortunately, because you are a visiting student researcher . . .

At this point, I go so far as to express a crumb of disappointment:

My reply, June 10

. . . I am somewhat dismayed . . . informed you of my status . . . if you'd have let me know in the first place that I was ineligible . . . three months have been lost . . .

There it was. I contacted whoever I could think of, while the Fulbright office made inquiries on my behalf. My best friend Petter's sister and brother-in-law, Inger and John Erik, who had lived in the area and had friends there. Peripheral contacts of my family. There was an activist network in Berkeley; Ed Roberts's mother was still alive and might have had a bungalow to rent.

The tone of the emails I received from the university grew gradually more perplexed. What was it that was so difficult for me? Couldn't I just figure something out at the International House? they wondered. Couldn't I just share one of the rooms there with my caregiver?

Aha—now I understood. The university had not realized that I planned to come *alone*. I had never said as much, and the notion had never been considered, since wheelchair users didn't travel alone, at least not abroad—did they? All of these small details that I had inquired about—an accessible bathroom, enough room for my wheelchair—seemed much less important if there was another person in the picture. A caregiver, someone who would follow me around all day, who would do all the things I couldn't do for myself. Someone who would act as my arms and legs.

This is how one becomes *a demanding person*: by asking for more than is offered. This is how one becomes *a problem*: by pointing out a problem.

The obvious question was the one never posed to me at all: *What makes you think that this can be done?*

It could be done. Later that year, I got to know students and guest researchers who had arranged their lodgings only a few days prior to, or even days after, their arrival. People who had traveled with a suitcase or two, trusting that something would open up. I smiled politely, and said how nice for them that something opened up.

I, on the other hand, traveled there like an immigrant from the 1800s. One electric wheelchair and one manual wheelchair. Two enormous suitcases, and as many spare tires and inner tubes as I could wrangle from the Technical Aid Center in Oslo—I still don't know what kind of irregular intentions the techs at the center imagined I might have for those supplies. And I brought Petter along too, whom I had known since we were four; one year later, I was his best man, six years after that he was mine. He brought his camera so he could photograph the sidewalks, curbs, and platforms for an accessibility project he was working on with the City of Oslo. He is as preoccupied as I am with centimeters and millimeters, with what is technically possible and impossible; he is an engineer.

We landed at San Francisco International Airport and called the number for the SuperShuttle. A breeze from the Pacific Ocean wafted quietly and hazily over the airport. A blue van with yellow writing on the sides drove up next to the arrivals terminal. The driver opened the side door of the van and folded out the lift. I had scheduled this transport ahead of time, after extensive online research had led me to conclude that SuperShuttle's were the largest vehicles. I rode the wheelchair into the truck and the lift folded back up. The wheelchair didn't fit, not by a long shot. Back out again, and the driver folded up one of the seats and rotated it in toward the wall. Almost, but not quite. I had a panicked feeling that the entire venture was going to end there, that we would have to fly back to Oslo immediately. In the end, we remembered that the basket attached to the back of my wheelchair could be removed. When we finally got the door closed, it was with half an inch of space to spare behind my wheelchair. But, it closed. Some things hinge on such tiny measurements. Twenty millimeters.

The time line splits, again and again. Each coincidence and each choice creates a new version. From an external perspective, everything that has taken place is the history of someone else; it can be seen from outside, evaluated more neutrally.

So much of my life can be interpreted as the predetermined result of the illness with which I was born. It can also be interpreted as having been determined by the country of my birth, by the parents I was born to. My privileges are no less real because they exist side by side with something else. In a way they are heavier, the gravitational force that they exert is stronger, they pull me in one direction and my illness pulls in another, two incompatible horizons of expectation.

It's easy to think of genetics as fate. I don't want this to be true, I have not wanted to allow myself to be limited by a mutation, it seems utterly ridiculous, such an infinitesimal alteration to one's genetic material, much too small to be measured in centimeters or millimeters. And yet, what could possibly determine the story of my life more than the very body that has lived through it?

I remember this: every time I traveled abroad, I was the only one.

There are photos of me from the film school days in Denmark, among a group of exchange students in Amsterdam and Utrecht, on campus in California, at a Fulbright gathering in Chicago. In all of the photos, I am immediately recognizable. I am most often found at the outer edges of the group, or else right up in front. There are practical reasons for this. I am at the bottom of the large stairway, a pendant to the composition. The large electric wheelchair does not integrate harmoniously into the picture.

Mari, who grew up in the house next to ours, also used an electric wheelchair. In school plays, the teacher wanted to hide it—and most of her—under a white sheet. The strange creature on stage became just as inexplicable, a disturbing spectacle. The head of a small girl, floating above an empty white field.

In San Francisco, at a gathering for international students from all over California, there was one other. A man, a few years older than me, in a manual wheelchair. I still regret that I didn't speak with him.

Sometimes, at the University of Oslo, there was a scooter parked where I usually parked my wheelchair outside of the lecture hall. Its owner and I studied in the same building for many years, we saw each other at concerts. We avoided meeting for the longest time. When we were subsequently introduced, through mutual friends, we found out that we had even attended the same high school. Our family backgrounds were also quite similar: culturally savvy, academic. It shouldn't have been a surprise; we were wheelchair users studying at the Faculty of Humanities after the turn of the century, and, as far as I am able to recall, there were only two of us.

I am not talking about surviving. I am not telling Mark O'Brien's story. I am not talking about becoming human, but about how I came to realize that I had always already been human. I am writing about all that I wanted to have, and how I got it. I am writing about what it cost, and how I was able to afford it.

I am trying to write myself out of others' language. I am trying to write myself out of the gaze of others. For each layer that I take away, the less certain I am that anything inside *can* be described. What would it mean to describe that which is unseen, which only exists for itself? There is an idea that our cognition plays out on an inner stage in front of some sort of tiny mental being representing our true selves. We seem to be unable to escape the notion that there is an *I* that is entirely distinct from our embodied self, that the *I* is really a kind of recording angel, trapped in the auditorium of our material skull.

I would like to think myself away from my body, away from my injured, worn ankles. But there is no me that exists apart from this body, in some unmarked form. That body would have lived an entirely different sort of life.

And yet it haunts me. It casts another kind of shadow. I shut my eyes and go skiing each winter, I run 10K each morning. I dash off to another country at a moment's notice, grab my carry-on, run out the door and hail a taxi, make my way quickly through the security check and sprint to the gate. I haven't made arrangements for where I'll stay when I arrive, I climb into a taxi and simply say: *Drive me somewhere I haven't been before.* I open my eyes.

Ida and I are parents together. In the summer, when Alexander is just over a year old, we visit his grandparents, my parents, at the house in Frøen where they still live. There are four of us adults, a good number for handling a small child who has learned to walk and wants to explore the ends of the earth. My mother walks around looking at the flowers and plants, there are currant bushes and gooseberries and raspberries in the garden. She and my father have planted two apple trees, one for Alexander and one for his cousin, who is about a year older.

My father carries Alexander on his arm, they walk around taking in the world's mysteries.

"Da-DAH!"
"Yes, that is an owl."
"DA-dah?"
"No, it's not alive, I don't think, it's there to scare away the other birds. But let's see."
"Da-DAH!"

There are traces of me in the house and garden, some small, some larger. The ramp that goes down into the garden from the veranda. The chair with a lift/lower function that can be rolled over to the coffee table. The platform lift at the main entrance, still in operation, almost three decades after it was first installed, thanks to persistent maintenance. The work never ends. One of the first times Ida came to dinner with me and my family, she witnessed my father stand and go outside, the meal hardly over, to defrost the lift's frozen control panel with a hair dryer.

I attend to my wheelchair as if to a vintage car, my ears twitch at every sound of dissonance, however minuscule, I am constantly checking the depth of the tread, and I feel the tiniest variations in the steering apparatus like a shiver up my spine. It's taken me a long time to be able to tell the difference between something that indicates the start of a mechanical failure and something that represents merely my own exhaustion.

There's always something, is one of my family's sayings. Another one is this: *Onward and upward.* These adages complement each other, in a way. The work is never finished, but that's no cause for despair. Hope lies with the results—however great or small—but the fight against entropy has its own intrinsic value as well.

I swam outside in California, in the swimming pool on the roof of Hearst Gym, beneath a blazing sun. The evenings of August 2008 had been chilly, as the fog seeped in across San Francisco Bay. It was the cold ocean wind, the damp mist, that made Mark Twain, or someone else entirely, go over the top: *The coldest winter I ever spent was a summer in San Francisco.*

In the warmth of autumn, I finally understood that I was truly there, on the other side of the globe. My blood circulation is slower than most. For as long as I can remember, I've had a chill from September to May. Now I was going around in T-shirts, a rarely needed hoodie in my bag. Every day I enjoyed a bagel at an outdoor café on the corner of College and Bancroft and watched the birds and squirrels eat crumbs and leftovers. They were unusually fat squirrels, sedate and confident. This was the gift I received, or was lent: another place, abundant in fat squirrels.

An elevator went to the roof of Hearst Gym. A small chair lift could be rolled over to the edge of the swimming pool. I was lowered slowly down into the water by the lifeguards; this went without saying. My legs were swallowed up by the sunlit water. Yet another layer of anxious expectation and disappointment was washed away. I swam in the cool water beneath the warm sun. The distance between thought and action was gone.

When I'm in the water, I daydream and remember. It's like the moment before falling asleep, when the body and thoughts detach and slowly drift apart.

Ida asks me, her voice incredulous: *But how do you remember that?* We haven't been together for very long, and *that* refers to the list of small things to be done around the house, remembering when the dryer should be switched on and off, when the grease filters in the range hood should be cleaned. But these things are easy to remember, I explain, compared to all of the big things. Because *that* also refers to how we are supposed to get from the airport in San Francisco to Berkeley, how we are supposed to get from Schiphol to Amsterdam.

Every trip contains hundreds of tiny steps, just as every movement can be broken down into many tiny components. I must picture all of them to myself in detail, I picture them as clearly as the situation necessitates, I lie awake at night picturing them, like Funes with his perfect memory. Borges once said that the story about the man who couldn't forget was in fact ("naturally") about insomnia. About being unable to let go of the world.

We are sitting on the sofa as we speak, and I move to stand and get a glass of water. Ida offers to get it for me, she offers to help me stand up. But I want to get up off the sofa myself. I have the ability to do it. All it requires is a bit of planning.

Ida says I'm a top-level athlete. Not because I have particularly well-developed musculature, but because the weak muscles that I have must be used so actively and deliberately, because I am worn out after a day of chasing the baby around the house, a day full of laundry, of food preparation, of completely ordinary, everyday tasks. This is my athletic training regimen, the average day is my sport, every trip from the sofa to the kitchen is a sprint, a deadlift, a marathon.

I know the pieces that comprise a movement. How the muscles pull together and the weight distributes. Which body parts extend outward and which ones balance them out. I can visualize the movement from beginning to end, from the initial moment of exertion until the sequence is complete.

We are sitting on the sofa and I begin to rise. Ida keeps silent, she knows this work requires concentration.

I inch up against the left armrest, not the right, position myself a small distance from the back pillow. The sofa is up against the wall so it will not slide backward.

I place my left forearm on the armrest and grasp the edge of it with my hand. My elbow is positioned precisely in the middle of the armrest, which will be significant in a moment. The sleeves of my shirt are rolled up, because there should be as much friction as possible, and it is essential that my skin be in contact with the sofa armrest.

Now I begin redistributing my weight. I turn over to the left and can see that my left elbow is the fulcrum of the spin where it is affixed to the sofa's armrest. My upper arm is at a ninety-degree angle to my forearm and the armrest. I maintain a firm grip on the sofa with my left hand. With my right hand, I grab ahold of the same spot.

Now comes the crucial moment: I place my right foot in line with the armrest and begin to shift my weight to my right calf, thigh, and hip. Here, I have to stop to check in with my body. If my right foot is positioned firmly enough on the floor, I may continue. If my left elbow is stable enough on the armrest, I may continue. If either my right foot or left elbow have slipped or are in the wrong position, I have to start over from scratch.

By degrees, I shift more and more weight to my right side and am now partially standing, my body tense. I am pushing my weight as much forward as downward, that is why it's important that the sofa is flush with the wall, so I won't push it away. My left knee now comes into play, I press it up against the seat cushion, against the frame of the sofa. My tension is more or less divided equally among three points, I am in an equilibrium of sorts. I stretch out my left arm, my left leg. My abdominal muscles are working, my shoulders are working.

It's at this point that my core muscles take over. I lift myself to a standing position. My left arm and left leg are now in a supportive role, their job is to stabilize, to maintain contact with the sofa. I assure myself that my balance is good. I breathe normally again. This is what it takes. Ida pulls her legs up onto the sofa softly so I have a clear path out to the kitchen, so I can walk out and fill up a glass of water. Another day, another routine.

But how do you remember that? Ida asked, and some years later we were planning Alexander's days together, his meals, his clothes, his nap times, without even recognizing that it was work, this is how much we had grown used to logistics. The work of planning came as naturally as breathing.

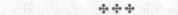

With such a way of being-in-the-world, planning becomes an automated habit, it becomes a reflex. I cannot think of an objective—grabbing a drink with a friend, say—without also considering the path to the objective, where we should go, whether there are steps up to the door, where the toilets are located.

This reflex has become a personality trait, a trait about which I feel ambivalent. Many wheelchair users that I know live in houses that are tidy, even spartan. This is simply a necessity if there's a chance that you might drive your wheelchair into an obstacle inside, getting helplessly lodged between this or that in your own living room. I understand it. I am able to walk a little, although I stumble easily, so clear, flat surfaces are crucial. This is another form of determinism—not genetic, but just as physical.

It's the same when transport services have to be arranged far in advance of planned travel, or when the majority of my questions are met with *No.* Personalities are formed in the space where inner needs meet external demands. I have a friend who stumbles and falls almost as easily as I do, but his house is not tidy, the floors are covered with toys and small objects. Is it the external demands that make us different, or the inner needs? Are there further imperative circumstances in my life, or is it that I am more sensitive to them?

Franz Kafka wrote, in "A Little Fable": *"Alas,"* said the mouse, *"the world gets smaller every day. At first it was so wide that I ran along and was happy to see walls appearing to my right and left, but these high*

walls converged so quickly that I'm already in the last
room, and there in the corner is the trap into which I
must run."
"But you've only got to run the other way," said the cat,
and ate it.

I am industrious; if I had been otherwise, I
would be in another place. I work in haste; if I
didn't, I would be nowhere. I wish to prove that
I'm as good as everyone else. But there is no final proof of this, not for anyone who has ever
lived. There is no end goal in life, and yet it's
human to think one exists. The teleological element, summed up by a theologian from another century:

We are quite naturally impatient in everything to reach **Pierre Teilhard**
the end without delay. **de Chardin**

It could have been different. I remember how
I thought about it. From the ages of ten to
twelve years old, I lived in the belief that once
I turned twenty, I would no longer be able to
walk. It seemed incredibly far off, that age of

being *an adult*, but this far off future nevertheless felt disconcertingly real.

I slept poorly then. This was due to anxiety
about the future, but also immediate physical
discomfort: I had to wear braces on my legs at
night, I was uncomfortable in bed.

My diagnosis came with cause for concern about
eventual problems with my back, legs, and overall musculoskeletal system. The solution in
those days, at the end of the 1980s—my childhood, yet another epoch—was to tighten, screw
in, counteract the body with metal and leather.
Stiff soles under the feet, pins and straps up
around the legs. The next pair of braces were
made of molded fiberglass, not as heavy, but
itchier, and they made me sweat. Both variants
were purported to prevent the muscles from
tensing in the wrong places. I went to bed at
night not to sleep, but to attend treatment.

A more lasting solution, the orthopedic surgeon's suggestion, was to cut the tendons of the
legs and fix the ankles at ninety-degree angles.
Dr. H put faith in the value of this operation.

Orthopedics: the art of straightening children out. Another body existed, a better version of my own and, with a little surgical help, mine could more closely resemble that other body.

In 1992, the year I turned eleven, I was used to wearing braces to bed, but not every night—it was a trial for me, for my father, for my mother. I slept poorly, or not at all, and we had to negotiate, to argue, without knowing for what or with whom we were negotiating, or even according to what premises we were arguing. We wanted to do the right thing, the sensible thing, that which would secure the best possible future for me, but the future was silent and invisible. Twenty-five years later, I know the answer. A few nights a week without braces, and I am still able to walk. My body is still my body.

The future no longer feels distant to me. When I write these words for the first time, Alexander is barely even a year old, but as I edit the manuscript, he is almost two. Tomorrow he will start school, the day after that he will be moving out on his own. To live with an infant in the house is to live from day to day, but the days slip by at an uncomfortable speed, the infant vanishes before our eyes, and now there's a little boy in his place. His pulls himself up more steadily today than he did yesterday, the muscles in his legs grow stronger and stronger. What if it had not been this way, what if his leg muscles had not kept up with the rest of him, what would we have thought then, which doctors would we have consulted, what advice would we have taken?

Clinical note, January 15, 1992

He sits and walks with somewhat raised shoulders and movements of motoric compensation as he did previously, but he still has generally good posture without the development of scoliosis.

[. . .]

Dorsal braces on his legs at night cause sleep disturbance so he is allowed to leave off some nights despite Dr. H's recommendations.

[. . .]

Conclusion: Practically speaking, stable condition over the past 2–3 years.

My parents used the word *skinner* to refer to the braces, it means *tracks* in Norwegian. I was six years old and imagined myself being tied to train tracks. I've placed this memory at the cabin that we borrowed from my uncle, on the island of Nøtterøy, where we went every summer, I don't think it's the right place, but that's how I remember it now. Every day, we did the exercises the physiotherapist had prescribed. My mother or father unrolled a red gym mat on the floor, and we did the exercises together. They extended my muscles, and I clamped and relaxed them so that the stretches would have maximum effect. Sitting in an upright position, I leaned against the wall and used my own weight to stretch my ankles, my legs; lying on the mat, I tried not to complain while my parents pulled my arm muscles, and together we tried to stagger the contractions. Exercises by day, braces by night. I was thirteen years old when we finally packed them away.

Leg braces have gone in and out of style over the years, just as stretching has gone in and out of style. It has been bittersweet to read about the attempts to find out whether these methods work, to guarantee what is known as *evidence-based knowledge*. It turns out that it is not easy to guarantee evidence-based knowledge about uncomfortable and uncertain treatment methods that must be implemented every single day, over the course of many years. Few people are willing to subject their children to decades of randomized, controlled experiments.

It may be—I must allow myself this thought—that the entire ordeal was a waste of time and energy. It may be it made no difference either way.

I still sleep poorly. Thoughts of the next day's tasks keep me awake. I think about every minute detail, I replan things I've already planned. I imagine how I will sit in the wheelchair, drive out to the garage, and get into the car, how long it will take, what could go wrong, maybe someone will have broken into the car during the night, maybe the battery has gone dead. I imagine that the taxi to the airport might never come, that my wheelchair won't be able to be transported to the airport, that I'll be forced to arrive in a new city without my wheelchair.

Just like Funes with his perfect memory, I am able to imagine innumerable scenarios, each of them different, but one scenario I am unable to imagine, that the airplane crashes, my brain spares me this one thought at least, and for that I am grateful. My work will be there in the morning. Onward and upward.

Around the same period of time, on the brink of puberty, I began to obsess over superheroes. They had absolute freedom of movement. Superman could fly. Spider-Man could swing from building to building. Unrestricted movement was always a superhero leitmotif. Their costumes were taken from circus artists, from acrobats and tightrope walkers. The great illustrators of the Silver Age—Jack Kirby, Steve Ditko—especially loved primary colors and bodies in flight.

There was another aspect that appealed even more to me. The superheroes had secret identities. The bodies they pretended to inhabit were not their real bodies. They could cast off their plain, everyday props—Clark Kent's glasses, Peter Parker's geeky teen wardrobe—and be free.

My ankles were never operated upon. The last time I looked into the possibility, some years ago, I was referred to a surgeon who said: *Wait.* There are no guarantees that such a procedure would solve anything, and several ways for new problems to emerge. *You walk in your own way,* said the surgeon.

I sway. I walk on the outsides of my feet, the weight falls on my soles, and my gait is stiff, I have poor balance. Ida and I clear the living room floor of toys several times a day, and I don't walk through a dark room without knowing that the path is clear, or without my cell phone's flashlight switched on.

But I walk. This is my body. It's familiar.

I don't have a secret identity. My costume, my everyday props, are with me at all times. I walk wearing custom-made footwear. Strictly speaking, they are such a tight fit on my feet, they are so stiffly supportive, that they are or- thoses. From a purely tactile perspective, they remind me of the braces. That feeling, of my toes bound tightly down to the soles, is exactly the same. It is a strangely claustrophobic sensa- tion, if I start to think about it, like being too aware of my own tongue and how confined it is resting in the narrow cavity of my mouth. My shoes are like plaster casts in which my feet are affixed. I wear them in winter and summer alike, out of doors and in the house.

But I walk. And each step brings me a quiet de- light. The soles of my shoes are as soft as they are supportive. I float on them, around about the world.

My diagnosis constituted a limit, the quiet mira- cle was that the limit moved slightly year by year.

I turned twenty, and still I walked, so the limit was pushed to twenty-five.

I turned twenty-five, and still I walked, so the limit was pushed to thirty.

I passed thirty. Something lifted. I began to believe that I could see past every limit, all the way to the horizon.

I have no fixed solution. I don't have another body for the purpose of comparison, I have only my own body.

Nor did my parents have any fixed solutions; they made their decisions to the best of their abilities. They had two children, one of whom had a rare muscular disease, a diagnosis that hardly anyone else had. They spoke with every doctor who would speak with them, and they spoke with each other, and they spoke with their child.

My feet continued to twist inward and downward in *equinus contractures* throughout my teens. And then they stopped twisting, more or less, and there they have stayed, more or less. For the past fifteen years I have been walking in shoes made from the same cobbler's lasts, copies of shoes that I ordered for the first time when studying in Amsterdam. Perhaps the wooden lasts will someday need to be modified, perhaps the contractures will get worse. I don't think it would help me to start sleeping in braces again. In any case, I would not do it.

One of the most difficult problems in robotics is simulating the human gait. It's easy to make a machine move. A motor can push a rod forward and back, and the energy from that motion can be transferred to a wheel. A gait is more complicated because it is ineffective, especially on two legs. A lot of energy goes into maintaining balance; otherwise, the machine topples over. It is an unstable and extraordinary manner of moving oneself.

You're walking.
And you don't always realize it,
But you're always falling.
With each step you fall forward slightly.
And then catch yourself from falling.
Over and over, you're falling.

Laurie Anderson, "Walking and Falling"

And the song has it right, most of the time. But sometimes you don't catch your fall, and a different realization takes place. I was a child who could not catch myself, I was always falling. For a while I wore a blue padded helmet, but that didn't last long, there are worse things than hitting your head, one of which is to be a child who is always walking around with a helmet on.

The question is, what can be done for, or with, a child who is constantly falling, who walks and then stumbles, who stumbles and gets hurt? Is this an acceptable condition, is this a risk one can live with? This is what must be decided, whether the risk is acceptable or unacceptable.

Note from
Dr. H,
May 8, 1995

The displacement of the feet has devolved significantly in the past years and this is the reason for the referral.
[. . .]
First and foremost is the question of operative treatment of the feet. I would recommend it, and think both feet could be operated on at the same time. He will wear a cast below both knees for 3 months post-op.
[. . .]
His parents, and Jan as well, are very anxious about the oepration [sic]. The father is particularly anxious about muscle breakdown following the operation and immobilization. I will not say that such a risk does not exist, but I think the risk of losing walking functionality

is greater if his feet displacement worsens than if we operate.

Life is a risky project. In November 2006, I broke my ankle. This happened in the back courtyard of the Oslo rock bar Mono, outside on the cobblestones, slick in the darkness of autumn. My wheelchair was parked in front, on the street. I was wearing the custom shoes from Amsterdam, the first really good pair of shoes I'd ever had. They gave me support up to my ankles, but the soles were hard and smooth, so that walking was like balancing on blunt stilts.

Once I had lost my balance, nothing else could happen but what happened. The weight of myself on myself caused two hairline fractures on the outside of my foot and two larger fractures on the inside. The *medial malleolus*: the *middle hammer*. In my memory, I hear a little bang as the hammer hits the cobblestones.

At first, I didn't understand what had happened. "Are you okay?" asked Trond, who was with me at the concert, who helped me get into my wheelchair. My foot hurt, I thought

I must have sprained it. That was irritating. I didn't know how I was going to get home again, how I would be able to walk around without shoes on. It was very painful. "Are you okay?" he asked again, and then I drove home in the wheelchair. I don't remember how I replied.

I removed my shoes in the bathroom, very carefully wiggled my foot into the sandals I wore to walk between the bathroom and bedroom. I was able to take a single step at a time if I held on to the doorframe and put as little weight as possible on my right foot. I have never been able to hop on one foot, but now there was no other way to get to my bed.

I thought to myself: *It's got to be better in the morning, it absolutely* has to be *better in the morning.* Ten years would pass until the next time I had to try so hard to force my will on the world, and that was the night my son was born.

I made it to the bed. And then, a few hours later, I needed to go to the bathroom. I don't remember how it went, how it was that I didn't fall, how I managed to get from the bedroom to the bathroom and back again with a broken ankle.

It *had to be* better the next morning, but it was not.

I lived alone and I woke up alone in my apartment. I pondered my options. There weren't many. I called my parents.

"We'll be right over," they said, or maybe what they said was even less than that because they were already on their way out the door. I didn't think about it then, but they had been prepared for this phone call since the day I'd moved away from home.

When I was living in Amsterdam, my parents were contacted by the Norwegian police, whose Dutch colleagues had apparently called regarding a car with the following registration number, did this car perhaps belong to their son? It turned out that an overzealous neighbor had reported a complaint; the permit that allowed me to park in that spot was not easily visible through the windshield. But for a tiny moment there, on the phone with the Oslo police, my parents conjured up images of my car sunk in the canal, of me under the water. Vulnerability is knowing how easily things can go wrong.

My parents came over. Together, they helped me to the bathroom so I could shower. Something terrible lingered in the air, we all knew that my ankle might be broken, we all knew what that would mean. I would not be able to walk without crutches. With both legs intact, my balance is already on a knife-edge. None of us said this out loud, it didn't matter. Instead, we went to the ER. The work continued.

For the next two months I was more helpless than I had been in twenty years. I moved back home. I rode around the house, in my childhood home, in a smaller electric wheelchair than I usually used. I went outside only once or twice over the course of those two months.

After six weeks, the plaster cast was removed, the fractures had healed correctly. We got ahold of a platform walker, a wheeled stand on which I could lean with my weight on my shoulders instead of my arms and hands, and take lurching steps forward, one by one. Then I went to the Cato Center and continued my rehabilitation there, in a warm-water swimming pool, with gentle strokes. I came back home, continued to use the platform walker, took ages to shower and even longer to get dressed. Spring came. I was able to take a few steps, wearing my shoes, with no additional support. It took months, half a year, but at some point, I was finally myself again.

While in the cast, I was unable to get out of bed and into my wheelchair on my own, I couldn't even shower without assistance. My father was the one who helped me, every day until the cast was removed and for many days afterward, until I regained two legs that worked as they had before. For two months I lived at home again, in my childhood home, a twenty-five-year-old man, and my parents and I had a glimpse of what could have been, of a very different life.

It could have been different. If I had reached the age of twenty-five without ever walking, always using a wheelchair, I would have been better acquainted with that reality, I would have *been* that body. I would have known what to do. This is what gets lost when a Norwegian politician, as sometimes happens, plops him- or herself down in a wheelchair and tries to wheel over tram tracks and down sidewalks, open heavy doors and navigate sharp curves. This pantomime of solidarity has nothing to do with a body's memory, with one's manner of being in the world. During those months spent at my parents' home with a broken ankle, all three of us functioned in a state of emergency, we traversed a foreign landscape.

And yet: it was a glimpse of the other future. A darker alternative, one which had always been there.

I am still able to walk. This is more important to me than it should be. I have read countless theoretical texts, critical analyses, and manifestos on the topic. What's so special about walking? What is it in our culture that has caused the health-care system to force people injured in car crashes through endless walking exercises for rehabilitation, even those who will never walk again, who might have been able to leave the hospital in a wheelchair in a matter of months rather than endure years of torturous training? What is it that makes people who walk *look down on* people in wheelchairs?

I don't know. But it's something. And I am still able to walk.

And yet: following my ankle break, I stopped getting out of my wheelchair when I was outdoors. This felt like removing a mask. I began to more readily ask people for help, and even more readily for an arm to hold on to, a shoulder upon which I could support myself. I gave up other things. I decided there were outdoor places where I was no longer willing to go, lines I was no longer willing to stand in.

It was around this time that I stopped going to clubs, or anywhere where dancing was the whole point. This was liberating, in a way, but it meant giving up the illusion that this was how I was going to meet a girlfriend, by acting as if I was like everyone else, only with a wheelchair parked outside at the curb.

It surprised me how painful this was. Not only that my ankle had to heal. I had an entire life narrative to reframe. It was during my rehabilitation that I applied for and was granted a fellowship for a project on disability. Only a few years earlier, I would have steered clear of such a topic. Now it was a way back to the question I had posed to myself but never answered: *Who am I in the world?*

From that period of half a year, during which I depended on my wheelchair almost exclusively, and when every single step was painful and merely a means to an end, something grew. It's not true that *whatever doesn't kill you makes you stronger*; on the contrary, whatever doesn't take your life can make you humbler, more willing to acknowledge your vulnerability. I hope this is what happened to me.

When I remember my childhood, I see all of those children who I did not become. There are countless versions of me, like in Borges's labyrinths, like in the story *The Garden of Forking Paths*. Some are more vivid than others. Sometimes when I am conversing with strangers, I begin to sense an itch, which turns into an impulse. Before I know it, I've mentioned something about how it is *at the university, where I work*.

"Oh, you *work*?"
And then, if the need has grown larger and more shameless, I reply: "Yes, I'm a professor."
"Oh. Oh, of course, there doesn't have to be anything wrong with your head even if . . . even if . . ."
No, there doesn't have to be.

They don't mean anything bad by it, these strangers. They are simply following the rules of thumb that we all follow. From a statistical viewpoint, I am a beneficiary of services granted to a disabled person. It's enough just to see the wheelchair; it's not proof, but it *is* a piece of evidence. More assumptions soon follow, other expectations are turned on their heads. I have a wife, a child? I think, I feel? I bleed if you prick me?

Well. I'm speculating here. The strangers are people too, I don't know what they are actually thinking.

I never attended a special needs school. Instead, I visited. My first physiotherapist worked there, at the low building next to the bigger, regular school. She worked with my body, helping to keep it in line.

I've gone to several physiotherapists in my life, a double-digit number of them. Too many to ever desire going again. If you aren't bringing them a finite problem, you yourself become the problem.

They are enthusiastic enough in the first months, they formulate what they call a *plan*. Then they start to notice that there are a lot of things about my body that don't change over time, and this is when their enthusiasm dissipates.

My arms are difficult to bend. They live a life entirely their own, they have found their own private angle. I began having my dress jackets tailored so that the arms are always slightly shorter than average, to accommodate the bend; in the closet the sleeves hang straight down.

When I was eighteen, I had a coat tailored for me from Follestad, it is still one of the most expensive garments I own. It was made of charcoal-gray wool and, through three different fittings, I experienced the entire tailoring process and all that it entails. At the first fitting, we learned that I have unusually straight shoulders; my shoulder blades turn slightly forward, but the top line of my shoulders is as straight as a ruler. The coat began to take shape. The pieces with horsehair reminded me of armor or a turtle's shell. My neck reminded me of a turtle's, where it projected forward from the tops of my shoulders.

It was an impractical coat, the fabric was heavy and yet it wasn't warm enough in the winter. Nevertheless, it was good to realize that the outside world could be adapted to me, could be shaped to fit my body like a glove.

It took a great deal of effort for me to get into the coat. My arms didn't bend enough. The best method was to guide my right arm all the way into the sleeve and then to hook my left underarm tightly enough onto the coat so that I could partly throw, partly wriggle it on. And then I was inside of it.

A few years ago, I stopped going to physiotherapy. I had considered this decision for a long time. I decided that none of the physiotherapists knew anything that I didn't already know. Each of us stood on the edge of the unknown; our routines and practices were nothing but rituals. It was surprisingly easy to give it up. I don't have enough time to spend it practicing rituals from someone else's religion, to fulfill a role determined for me by others. I am still on my way into the unknown, but at least I am headed in the direction of my own choosing.

Some role models do exist. Although there were several things I liked about *The West Wing*, the best was the way President Bartlet put on his jacket. He would sling it over his head and around his back, like it was a cape and he was headed into battle. I instinctively knew what I was seeing, and the actor confirmed it:

I was born under very difficult circumstances. They used a forceps and it smashed my left shoulder so I have very limited use of my left hand.

Martin Sheen

This quote demonstrates good language, well-chosen words. They are the words of one who has spoken them many times before, who knows what can be conveyed and what cannot be conveyed. My shoulder was smashed. Now I put on my jacket in my own way.

I wore my tailor-made coat for seven years. Then I finally conceded that it wasn't warm enough. Less energy is required when seated than when walking, and so one gets colder more easily. Still, I waited for seven years before buying a parka.

I have discovered something. My ankles are locked into their preferred position. My musculature is asymmetrical. My biceps are much stronger than my triceps. The back side of my thigh muscles are correspondingly much stronger than the front side. The tendons in my legs contract, as do the tendons in my arms. This is why I must plan how to get up off the sofa. I must guide a marionette whose strings are either too short or too long. I am completely tense. But this is my body. These movements are my movements.

At some point or other I stopped feeling uncomfortable about speaking with doctors. At some point or another I stopped speaking with doctors if there wasn't a concrete, limited problem they could help me with. At some point or another I stopped thinking about myself as someone who needed repairing.

I want something I cannot have. I want a different world. I don't know what that would look like. I want a world that is more open, more free. I want there to be space for me and all those I love.

Alexander is not yet one year old as I write this. We have only just begun to know him. Both of us know him better than any other person. He could not have been anyone other than himself, and yet he could have been, there could have been someone else in his place, if the dice had landed differently.

For us, for Ida and me, he is something beyond and prior to language. He is a physical presence of cosmic significance, he pulls words toward him and swallows them up in his gravitational field. The only thing to escape his event horizon is his own face, his grin.

How would we describe him if we weren't his parents? What language would we use? In my office there is a three-foot-long shelf of paper records full of descriptions. I have enough examples of the neutral language, the objective language. I read the same sober phrases again and again.

3-year-old boy, dark blond with brown eyes, attractive and well-proportioned, cracile [sic] with a generally lean physique, relatively poorly developed musculature but

Clinical note,
June 12, 1984

good posture. The boy shows clinical signs of neuromuscular disease, most likely myopathy with signs that all muscle regions are affected.

This is how it could be viewed, this is how it could be described. The clinical child, the child as *a case*. The papers in my office are meticulously ordered. I can follow the changes up through the years. The clinical language blends seamlessly with the bureaucratic. It marks the start of an endless dialogue with Social Services about how a life shall be lived.

One of the patterns in the dialogue consists of the following: my parents request something, their request is denied, they appeal the denial, they win. This process takes them several months, or years. They are too ambitious, too demanding. They ask for too much. They expect the impossible: something resembling a normal life.

The patterns run alongside and on top of each other: declarations and explanations woven into letters, letters referred to in other letters, chains of correspondence inquiring about inquiries, meetings and discussions referenced, speech condensed to writing, life condensed to text.

Another pattern arises when the state requests clarifying information. This pattern is repetitive and minimalistic because the requested details and information are always the same, over and over again, year after year after year. Case notes must be reviewed again and again, specific needs must be documented, situations described. The patterns grow more complex, more baroque. They expand like frost on the windowpane, like fractals, their details spreading ornately as they harden. The papers in my office comprise a particular device, an infernal text machine that can only be stopped in one way.

The Social Services Office has registered that you are the legal guardian of JAN GRUE.

Letter from Social Services, October 15, 1993

Letter from Social Services, February 11, 1999

We request information regarding: the needs for assistance and supervision at the present time.

✤ ✤ ✤

Letter from Social Services, December 5, 1996

We request information regarding the status of health at this time, regardless which doctor is handling him.

✤ ✤ ✤

Letter from Social Services, March 10, 1994

We request information regarding the status of health at this time, regardless which doctor is handling him.

✤ ✤ ✤

Letter from Social Services, March 10, 1993

In connection with recent updates, it may be necessary to gather new medical information. We therefore request the name and address of your attending physician.

✤ ✤ ✤

Letter from Social Services, February 7, 1991

In connection with recent updates, it may be necessary to gather new medical information. We therefore request the name and address of your attending physician.

✤ ✤ ✤

At the inquiry of The National Insurance Court, the father of the appellant claimed over the phone that the appellant has not wet himself, neither days nor nights, since turning three.

Verdict of the Social Services Tribunal, December 23, 1987

These patterns, these repetitive, subtly variable patterns, like a progression in a Bach fugue, have a mesmerizing effect when viewed over time, from the outside. They create an impression of *stasis*, of stagnation and permanence, alongside time as it passes, and life as it is being lived. It's this tension that makes me think of Bach, and about the endlessly rising canon from *Musikalisches Opfer*. As Douglas Hofstadter wrote about this piece, in his book *Gödel, Escher, Bach*: *By moving upwards (or downwards) through the levels of some hierarchical system, we unexpectedly find ourselves right back where we started.*

A diagnosis is a diagnosis is a diagnosis, a need is a need is a need, precisely because they must be confirmed again and again, just as a witness statement has to be recorded several times in order to confirm whether the witness has changed their story, to confirm whether there is a lack of consistency in the version of the story served up to the authorities.

At the same time, life is lived outside of letters, throughout the 1980s, throughout the 1990s. The music plays on.

I try picturing it to myself now, initiating a conversation with public entities, a conversation that will last for several decades. A conversation initiated by a clinical description of Alexander, a diagnosis, repeated over and over again, year after year.

Me: Tell me! Who are you?
The Voice: Me.
Me: That doesn't clarify things. *What* are you?
The Voice: The great and powerful Social Services.
Me: So, serve me!
Social Services: You have to take the long way, Grue. Go roundabout.
Me: No! Let me pass! (*Kicking and swinging.*)
Social Services: I'm Social Services, Grue, roundabout is the only way.

It is Social Services that is invulnerable, and Social Services that is injured. Social Services that is dead, and Social Services that lives.

. . . and so on. Back and forth are equally far, out and in are equally narrow.

Obviously, my parents didn't know what the next part of the dialogue would be, what would be the next scene in the play; they had never played this game before. The future was unknown, as the future always is.

We can't know what kind of life Alexander will lead, we cannot know what will happen next year, or tomorrow. The patterns become apparent over time, letters are mailed out one by one. One letter at a time, we internalize the bureaucratic language, the clinical language, first my parents, then me. We become masters at it. In my family we don't go roundabout.

On one rare occasion I dream there's nothing wrong with me at all. It was all just a misunderstanding. I only need to exercise a bit more. Then I'll grow stronger. I'll no longer need the wheelchair. There's nothing wrong with me.

❖ ❖ ❖

There *is not* anything wrong with me. So, where does this idea come from? What is it that casts this shadow?

Erving Goffman   *The stigmatized individual tends to hold the same beliefs about identity that we do; this is a pivotal fact.*

To acquire an identity is to learn to resemble someone else, to learn that one is different from someone else. If I want to know who I was meant to be, it's because I want to measure the distance to the person I have become. I want to know how far I've traveled.

Goffman's concept of stigma is tightly connected to shame, and shame is connected to existential displacement. In order for the stigma to work, it's necessary that both the person who is stigmatized and the society around that person—the normal people—are in agreement that this person is not how they ought to be. Shame attends the internalization of this sense that something is fundamentally wrong or is not as it should have been. When life is lived on false premises. It is this shame that I would like to write out of myself now, it is this that I would like to scrutinize, and cast off.

Stigma cannot be eliminated through action (even if you can camouflage it, or suppress it) for the simple reason that its root is not in what one does, but in *who* one is. It is who one is, or who one is perceived to be, that shapes the framework for how our actions are interpreted, so that even the most innocent acts can take on a shameful dimension. When I take care with how I dress, when I make sure to keep my wheelchair clean, when I take pains to behave *correctly*, it is, in part, because I know how other signals, other traits, will be interpreted.

It could have been different. My old, reliable, conformist strategies are not the only reality that exists. I could have been angrier, I could have been one of the activists. I could have chained myself to something, screamed at the top of my lungs.

But I don't want to be a bother.

What comprises *resistance*? Another language, another attitude. Telling it straight, without shame. My life is different from the lives of many others. It is just as fully my life.

With these words, with this book, I am creating a space in the world. If I succeed, I will be re-creating a part of the world, my part, with this book, with these words.

Creating space is difficult. The world does its best to resist.

Lawrence Weschler   *If I were somehow to be forced to write a fiction about, say, a make-believe Caribbean island, I wouldn't know where to put it, because the Caribbean as it is is already full—there's no room in it for any fictional islands.*

Dropping one in there would provoke a tidal wave, and all other places would be swept away.

For many years I wrote short stories about impossible things, stories that staged absurd ideas. This was also a form of resistance, and a form of practice. It was a test of boundaries.

The fictionalist has to be capable of tsimtsum, *of breathing in, of allowing—paradoxically, of creating—an empty space in the world, an empty time, in which his characters will be able to play out their fates.*

Lawrence Weschler

There is no fiction, regardless of how absurd it may seem on the first reading, which is not, if it is good, relevant to real people living in the real world.

The contact and the habit of Tlön have disintegrated this world. Enchanted by its rigor, humanity forgets over and again that it is a rigor of chess masters, not of angels. Already the schools have been invaded by the (conjectural) "primitive language" of Tlön; already the teaching of its harmonious history (filled with moving episodes) has wiped out the one which governed in my childhood; already a fictitious past occupies in our memories the place

Jorge Luis Borges

of another, a past of which we know nothing with certainty—not even that it is false.

This is where it ends, because this is where it begins: I dream of another world.

It is a world that, naturally, has space for wheel-chairs and for those of us who use them. It is a world in which we are not anyone's problem (a problem that no one in fact wishes to solve). It is a world through which I may move without bumping up against edges or being stopped by hindrances. A free-flowing world.

I must not spend too much of my time dreaming. If so, I wake up and feel sad. I try to locate the feeling of free flow in my waking hours too.

The closest I have come to another world is California, with its wide streets, its gently sloping ramps, its open, sun-drenched landscape. But beneath the sun, in San Francisco and in Berkeley, there are dozens of homeless people in dilapidated manual wheelchairs, with open sores on their feet, the accessible galleries and restaurants and university buildings are not for them, they are only open to a person like me, someone who flies in from abroad, still tightly tied to the umbilical cord of the Norwegian welfare state.

No. The closest I have come to another world is my family. The one into which I was born and the one I have received as a gift. The one I have been gifted is the one I have created. It is a fiction, it is an empty space in the world. Breathe in.

Any fiction that has been sufficiently conceived is already infused with reality. As soon as a new world becomes detailed enough for a person to inhabit, it also acquires its own problems and politics.

In any given culture and at any given moment, there is always only one "episteme" that defines the conditions of possibility of all knowledge, whether expressed in theory or silently invested in a practice.

Michel Foucault

It is almost impossible to think one's self out of the world as it is; this is what Foucault is writing about. We are trapped in our contemporary thought patterns, our contemporary behavior patterns. *This* is a wheelchair user, *this* is a wheelchair.

And Georges Couthon, what kind of wheelchair user was he, in the days of the revolution, what did he think about himself?

And Mark O'Brien, born barely one generation before me, who wrote that he became human late in life, what did he think about himself?

Michel Foucault *I wish I could have slipped surreptitiously into this discourse which I must present today, and into the ones I shall have to give here, perhaps for many years to come.*

✢ ✢ ✢

Enough theory. The discourse I am presenting is the discourse about my life. Life is *praxis*. The movement is a gradual coming together. Over the years, I have come to know my own body. I have learned to like it. I know my own limits, which are gradually being transformed into premises. Breathe in.

I conduct lectures and readings from my wheel-chair. The seat is mounted on a turntable. I can park sideways, but swivel to face the audience and stretch out my legs, crossing them almost casually. I speak more slowly than I am used to, I allow the sentences to rest in themselves, in their own weight. If what's in the background is quiet, what takes place in the foreground can be quite small, it can be subtle, and yet it has the power to captivate an entire room. Breathe out.

I am sitting on the sofa, Alexander comes over to me. He knows that Ida is the one who runs after him, he is the one who runs to me. Breathe in.

I half-sit on, half-stand at the tall barstool in the kitchen. Alexander is able to climb up into my arms, first he clings to my legs, then he grabs ahold of the edge of my sweater, and then he is up on my hip, and I am holding him. He is up close to me now, now he can show me the yellow dishwashing gloves that are on the kitchen counter, it is important for him that I see what he sees, see how nice they are. Breathe out.

Long after Ida and I became a couple, she recounted the first time we met, the way she remembered it. In the fall of 2009, we both began classes at a writing school run by Aschehoug publishing house. For a whole year, we would all spend one evening a week discussing nonfiction.

I had applied to the program because I wanted to do something new. Two months earlier, I had returned home after my year in California. I had changed over the course of that year. I didn't know quite what had happened to me, I didn't have the words for it. Something was different about the way I moved, my body language, my approach to life. I was changing, that much I knew, but I did not know where I was headed.

It was early fall, and we gathered outside on the plaza cobblestones at Sehesteds plass. We were waiting to be let in through the iron gate and the two bulletproof glass doors of the publishing house. I had once heard that Dag Solstad decided to be published by Aschehoug because the big door at Gyldendal, the publishing house across the plaza, was too heavy for him to open. I don't know if that's true, but I can certainly sympathize. These days, Gyldendal, my Norwegian publisher, has automatic doors and a universally accessible building. Aschehoug has five steps up to the ground floor.

I was well acquainted with these steps; when I began at the writing school in 2009, a novel I had written had been rejected on both sides of Sehesteds plass. For reasons that remain unclear, I thought that writing nonfiction would be easier. If I couldn't create *art*, at least I could write something that was *true*. That's how this book got its start. It's been ten years, one novel, and several short stories since then. That's how hard it is to write about the truth, about what has, in fact, happened. Breathe in.

This has, in fact, happened:

In Sehesteds plass, I sat there in my heavy wheelchair, which had been flown across the Atlantic Ocean and back. California lived within me. The eucalyptus trees in Berkeley seemed closer than the ground floor of the Aschehoug building, five steps up from the street.

Ida recounted her memory of that afternoon. It was similar to mine. She had seen me, seen the heavy, large wheelchair, seen the stairs that were the only way up to the room where our course was to be held. She was worried on my behalf. She saw the same problem that I did, the same stone stairway. Others have, in similar situations, seen *me* as the problem. *I* have seen myself as the problem. This has also happened. Breathe out.

Had this taken place a few years earlier, I would have tried to walk up the five steps without anyone's help. I would have insisted on it. I would have leaned up against the wall, placing my weight on one leg, angled my other leg up, pushed off, and hoped for the best. I would have tried to avoid eye contact. Only if I was unsuccessful would I have accepted help, and I would have done it against my will, moodily.

But now, I looked around at the group on the plaza and greeted everyone. There were two men there who were about the right height, both were four to eight inches taller than me. I asked them to help when the doors were buzzed open, allowing us to enter the building. I explained exactly what they had to do. One of them took my bag and both positioned themselves on either side of me. I put my arms around their shoulders. Then they lifted me as I took the steps one at a time, slowly and carefully. When we were at the top, I held on to them—*Wait a sec*—while I found my balance—*Okay, just like that . . . Thank you both.* And then we all went into the room where our course was to take place. Ida had watched what happened; she saw that I had a plan, and the plan was to ask for precisely the kind of help that I required. This impressed her, she told me.

It's often as simple as that. Other people like to help. They don't know how exactly, but they're willing. Some of them are good at lifting, others are not as good. Some of them keep their distance, others are stiff and nervous. This is not what I need. I need someone who gets up close enough to recognize where I am weak and where I am strong, which direction I'm able to bend if and when I am in the process of losing my balance. It often comes down to chance, but those who are best at supporting me are often those who have small children, who are used to carrying someone else, used to bodies that are weaker than their own. Breathe in.

It's often as difficult as that. Adults should not ask strangers for help, at least not the kind of help that brings them in close enough contact to smell one another's sweat. This is too intimate, it is reminiscent of something else. It crosses a boundary that exists for a reason, it opens the door to the liminal space.

It was up to me. It was always up to me. It took a long time for me to understand that passivity is another socially visible disposition. I had to learn that I didn't need to be passive because I was less mobile than others. Living in California helped. I learned to smile. I learned to use my voice better. I learned to take charge. Breathe out.

It was not only up to me. It was never only up to me. Our becoming occurs in the small parts we play every single day, in *this* scene, and in *that* scene. Erving Goffman attaches great importance to these theatrical performances in the process of understanding what we like to call *personality*, as if this is something with a constant size. It may be that we all have an inner core such as this, a constant inner *I*, but what does it mean if this *I* is kept hidden?

A person who plays a role each day *is* that role; if the mask is never removed, it becomes the face. We may assert that we are, in reality, something other than what the world sees, that we have hidden traits, that we are unseen heroes. We might even believe it ourselves. But what does that matter without external recognition?

When Ida entered a relationship with me, she took on my stigma at first. It manifested differently for her than it did for me. She became the recipient of questions that no one had ever asked me. A thousand tiny questions about what kind of couple we were, ranging from politely interested to pryingly, falsely concerned. How do you travel on vacations, how do you cook together, how do you have sex with someone who can't walk, does the wheelchair come up into the bed? (Children ask questions out of genuine curiosity, but it's the adults, with their entangled motives, who are able to evoke the truly surreal images.)

All of these tiny questions have tiny, trivial answers. Most lives, regardless of circumstances, are lived out in trivial spaces. The big question, the only one not asked, is: Why did you *choose* to take on this stigma, the one about which we are now reminding you? And the answer to *that* question is too big to give to strangers.

A person who is stigmatized knows it with her whole body. It means being vulnerable, being open to any manner of question, however uninformed, however intrusive it may be.

A person who is stigmatized shies away, because nothing good can come from meeting the gaze of others, of those who are normal.

Stigma functions like a kind of radio static, white noise sent out over every channel. If you wish to push your way through, you have to know the frequency, you have to know what kind of signals you are sending, and how to strengthen them. This takes experience.

In the United States, I made an attempt at online dating. This term—*online dating*—already seems as antiquated as *calligraphy* or *courtship*. I write *This was before Tinder* and with that, the written moment becomes fixed in time too. I made an attempt at online dating, and among multiple disappointments and some bright moments I learned an important thing: the body cannot be concealed. The wheelchair cannot be thought away.

And yet, this is precisely what I wanted to do, as if eradicating the symbol was enough to change what was symbolized. Self-portrayal invites camouflage, the use of smoke and mirrors, but there are limits to what can be camouflaged, and some forms of stigma are reinforced the more you try to hide them. To not mention the wheelchair would indicate shame; to allow a sneak peek of it at the edge of my profile picture could send conflicting messages. *A wheelchair? What wheelchair? Oh, that wheelchair? Yes, now that you mention it, it does happen to belong to me, yes, I don't think about it very much. You see, it was just sitting there outside my door one day, looking a little forlorn, so I took it in and it's been parked in the entryway ever since.* I might as well have posted a picture of myself seated in the wheelchair with a white sheet covering it and my entire body.

One of the women I met through online dating in the U.S. told me I was an exhausting conversationalist. She felt I had exposed her to *a relentless sociological interview.* I had asked her so many questions that there was no time for any of hers. Which was also the point. At the end of the evening we kissed, and that quiet moment housed the open and obvious message: this was a parting kiss.

This happened several times. Slowly, I began to learn that there is something that lingers after the words. Slowly, I learned that my body, even if not like all the others, was able to communicate signals just as clearly. I had only to become better acquainted with it, and to get to know it in a language other than the clinical language.

I avoid certain words in what I write, there are words I could have used but did not use. I do not want to be a *case*, an example to follow. I don't want Ida and me to be in this role, even if we often are. It's partly our own fault; we have sought the attention. But this is because we are visible whether we would like to be or not, we are hypervisible, we cannot hide ourselves within the crowd.

Our life together is not an illustration, it is not a demonstration of any moral or philosophical point, we are not the solution to an ethical dilemma.

This battle is lost no matter which words I use or do not use. I am too many things, I make for too good an example. I am a wheelchair user and father, I am an author and academic. I am always an example already, and so, by proxy, is my partner, the person with whom I have had a child. She has been informed of this since day one, informed in a skeptical, worried tone: *How . . . brave of you.*

I write, as simply as I am able, about what has happened. I don't end by changing *is* to *ought*. I write about our lives together, without undertones. Our life, in all its simplicity.

There was a time when I did not know what or who I was. I lacked categories that were my own. My impression of myself was formed by many encounters and just as many expectations. I didn't know what kind of body I was.

I didn't know what kind of body I was because I lacked a story. There are a lot of stories about children who are weak or sickly. And almost inevitably, one of two things happens: they get better, or they die. They are either ugly ducklings or steadfast tin soldiers.

But what about those of us who grow to adulthood but remain weak? What happens to those of us who continue living our strange lives, who remain in our otherness, those of us who don't have the decency to conform to the proper narrative patterns?

We have no key. No map. We must try out various strategies one by one and know that we will fail over and over again, with no guarantee of anything more.

We lack role models, there's no one to tell us how to be lovers, partners, parents.

There is a freedom in this, but it is an overwhelming freedom, it is an open, frozen expanse. *Terra incognita.*

When I met Ida, I had a better idea of myself than earlier in my life. And still I began, almost unwillingly, to tread down old paths. I now saw myself through her gaze, externally. It was uncomfortable. I saw what I had come to accept, what adaptations I'd had to make. I began to see more clearly the contours of the forces that had shaped me, what things were not merely a given, what could have been different. And so, we began treading down new paths, together.

The first time we traveled out of the country together, to Denmark, was a dress rehearsal of sorts. The grand performance was half a year after that, when I knew that we were a couple and I wanted to introduce her to California. We needed the dress rehearsal, there was a lot we still didn't know about each other. We had known each other for a year by that point, but had spent almost all of our time in the same neutral settings, the same classroom at Asche-houg publishing house. It was something else entirely to move around together, it was something else to be a pair, out in the world.

At the airport, she walked away from me out of habit. We had checked in my big, heavy wheelchair as special baggage. It was a time-consuming, boring procedure. We'd had to wait in line to speak with someone at the counter. This was already unusual, I recognized. The departure hall at Gardermoen has a self-service baggage drop-off machine. Standing in line to get to the counter where we could speak with someone put us in the same group as parents with small children, the digital illiterate, and travelers with large, cumbersome pets.

Our turn at the counter lasted fifteen minutes. First, my information had to be recorded, the same information I had given when I ordered the tickets, but airlines have bad memories, if it suits them. And then a half hour passed as I waited for the service attendant from spe-cial baggage who could explain to the person at the counter how to handle 450 pounds of complicated mechanics and electronics. I never arrive at the airport less than two hours before my departure, regardless of my destination. I am unable to hurry.

My own wheelchair vanished into the baggage area, followed by my quiet prayer that it would arrive in one piece. We were then given a manual wheelchair to borrow. Ida wheeled me over to the security checkpoint. It was the first time she had wheeled me, and there was a peculiar sense of intimacy associated with that act. My arms are not strong enough to push the wheels of a manual wheelchair, and even though I am not as helpless as a child when seated in one, I still feel incredibly vulnerable. I can be steered any which way by someone else, I can be wheeled and parked in various places, which has happened, on other occasions, at other airports. I have watched children who lean forward in their strollers, clutching at the frame and rocking their bodies, *faster, faster.* I feel empathy with them.

It was after we had gone through the baggage check that Ida walked off and left me sitting there. She was used to the fact that I was able to move on my own, that in my wheelchair I was able to move as automatically and naturally as anyone on foot.

When I called out to her, I had a bad conscience, because I knew how embarrassed she would feel, but also because it was like poking a hole in a great big, floating soap bubble. Inside the bubble, we could be like any other couple.

We are not like any other couple, far from it. We are us.

After a few minutes, Ida was able to laugh at the whole thing. We were farther along, we were on the airplane now, we were in the air. We still haven't really landed yet, perhaps—I can hope—we may never need to land.

But there was another side to the situation, and that was how angry Ida became at seeing me in transit, at seeing how I was treated. When we arrived in Copenhagen, no one was there waiting with a manual wheelchair for us, in spite of the fact that we had ordered one in advance, in spite of their assurances that one would be waiting. The assistance personnel asked if I couldn't just possibly walk up to the golf cart they had parked at the gate. They asked this question in a tone that was part resignation, part command. I knew this tone well. It is often employed by service people who don't like their jobs, but who also don't want to worry about criticisms from dissatisfied customers. If a wheelchair user stops flying because the whole ordeal is too uncomfortable, too much work, their choice makes life easier for the rest of the world.

The tone expressed that this request, for the provision of a wheelchair to move up the sky bridge, couldn't really be necessary. Ida looked at me incredulously as I explained that yes, in fact, it was. She held back her outrage as they begrudgingly went and got a wheelchair and wheeled me up to the golf cart parked at the gate. When no one moved to help me out of the wheelchair and into the golf cart, it was she who helped me. This was business as usual for me, this was simply what it meant to travel. I was very familiar with the waiting room at

Kastrup, the room where *passengers requiring assistance* are deposited to wait for their flights, for however many hours there are to wait. There is nothing but a toilet and drinking fountain in the waiting area, it is a Beckett-like space.

This was not a familiar world to Ida, and her outrage, I believe, was the natural response to it. The reasonable response. However, it is not a reaction that can be maintained over thirty years, it is not a feeling that can live in your body for so long without it harming the body.

When we traveled to Bordeaux some years later, we changed flights in Charles de Gaulle, which would be the world's second-worst airport if its employees hadn't bumped it up to the all-time worst. We had to wait a long time for assistance, and when the employee had finally come to get us, we had to wait for another half hour while they took a cigarette break. They paid us only partial attention, the amount you might pay a suitcase set down a few arm's lengths away. The most important thing was that they didn't lose us. When they tried lifting me out of the white, rust-flecked Renault, which shuttled at uneven intervals between the terminals, they dropped me on the ground.

When we traveled to the Netherlands, the employees gave us a hard time because we had not informed them, in advance and preferably by letter, about which train we had planned on taking from Schipol to Amsterdam so that they could unlock the ramp down to the train tracks. This procedure took only three minutes but required, according to the personnel, a minimum of twenty-four hours' advance notice.

Ida's reaction to this, her barely suppressed rage, forced me to see what was actually going on. She forced me to see, again, how bizarre it was to be handled like a piece of freight, like a logistical problem, like an intrusive element. Bizarre that it was bizarre, because I had also seen it clearly, at times. Of course I had, this was how I had been traveling all my life. I had merely come to learn that this was a given, that it was ordinary, that it was the way of the world. That is the price you pay. You cannot live in an uninterrupted battle with the entire world; I cannot. Ida expressed the outrage that I had always felt but was never able to express, she released it for me. And we continued planning our trips together, we knew that, no matter what happened under way, we would feel the airplane lift off from the ground, we would take flight together.

I thought I knew who I was, Ida. I thought I knew what I was. You helped me to take another look.

When we first began dating, Ida was cautious about asking me the normal questions. How many girlfriends I'd had. Who was my first. She knew it was a sensitive topic, perhaps too sensitive, because I was reserved, almost evasive. This was, in part, because I did not yet know which story I wanted to tell her.

One story was a variation on *the normal story.* The first time I kissed someone, the first time I slept with someone. A few funny anecdotes, a few stories to shine the light a bit more on who I was, in a conveniently flattering light. And this

was a story I was able to tell. It was not untrue,
it was just a bit *thin*.

The other story was about this very aspect, the
thinness. It was about longing and hunger. About
what had been different for me, and why. It was
about many things I was not yet ready to discuss, not while I was in love, not while I was
enjoying myself. My happiness, then and there,
was overwhelming. I got dizzy looking back at
the past, with the vertigo you feel when realizing
just how far down it is to the ground.

I was careful about which questions I posed to
Ida. I considered which questions she might ask
in response. I was afraid of losing face, of being
exposed. Of her sudden discovery that I sat in
a wheelchair.

I used to dream about leaving everything behind.
Of going off on travels without luggage, leaving
my clothes lying on the beach, swimming out to
sea. Or else of walking along the streets in a foreign city, most often Paris, ducking into a café,

ordering a glass of wine, sitting anonymously, no wheelchair in sight.

Why these two particular images of freedom? Because both reflected the impossible inherent in the possible. Because they were not so very far away, I had only to shut my eyes to sense the smells, the tastes, the anonymity, the loneliness. These were melancholy images.

When we became a couple, Ida reminded me that she had never been to Paris, that before we were together she had been out of the country only a handful of times, whereas I had lived for long periods in Denmark, the Netherlands, the U.S. There were many privileges I had never seen as privileges; this is inherent in the word.

I went to school, then I went to university. In my own country, in another country, and then in a third country.

I got a job, I got another job. I felt like a comic book figure who has run off the edge of a cliff. It's only when you look down that you become in danger of falling. Keep moving forward, don't stop, don't look down. Work is focus, work is freedom, show that you are as good as everyone else, show that you're just as productive, show that you are like them, even if you aren't, *do it*, whatever the cost.

I met you, Ida.
We got married.
We decided to have a child.

I write these words for the first time one week before the due date, I expect to hear it at any moment, that it's time to call the hospital, that we will have to leave soon.

I rewrite these words half a year later, Ida is out of the house with Alexander bound up on her back, she says that she carries him like a Sherpa would. He lies against her back, grinning while she ties him up in the wrap, he knows where he is and that he is safe.

I write them a third time, another year later, when Alexander is in daycare, Ida is at the office. We aren't rookies anymore, we've become parents together. We have learned from day to day what we can do and what we cannot do.

Three people enter and leave our house, at different times of day, when I take Alexander out or bring him home, one of them is always with me. They are not my arms and legs. I have my own arms and legs. They are my helpers, they help me. They pick Alexander up off the ground and help him to settle on my lap, they help me to pull on his play outfit. We go out into the world together.

Was it different for us to have a child? Can one birth be compared to another?

Five days after the due date, we were certain it was time.

It was the middle of the night. Ida had been having contractions for several days. There was supposed to be a noticeable difference between the contractions and labor pains, but how can you tell the difference between things you have never experienced? You see a big creature in the dark, and it might turn out to be some other big creature in the dark.

We called the clinic. They advised us to wait— *It's better if you stay home, try to take it easy*—but they also said we could come, if we wanted.

This was part of our agreement. They knew things were different for us. We couldn't flit around as quickly as other couples might be able to, we weren't able to play out one of those scenes from a rom-com in which everything comes down to the last second, where he packs her into the car in the eleventh hour with paraphernalia strewn everywhere, a scene in which it all turns out well in the end, in spite of everything. If things turn out well for us, it's because we have planned it down to the last, tiny detail, we've thought through what is going to happen, action by action and consequence by consequence.

In these ways we are like other couples: for the last week, we weren't alone in our apartment.

Mari, Ida's best friend, moved into the guest room, which would soon be turned into a nursery, the night after the due date. It was from this point on, when the contractions started to get serious, that we knew we needed her. Mari was there to support Ida when she was dizzy, it was Mari who could accompany Ida in a taxi when things got urgent. We could have ordered a taxi that would be able to take me and my wheelchair, but we had no way of knowing when it might show up, in ten minutes or in an hour. We needed another plan.

The due date came and went. We ordered take-out and watched B-list movies. Took a vacation in our own living room and pretended to return to everyday life. We were teenagers again, the only thing we had to do was wait for a new life to start, without a clue what that meant.

In the middle of the night, the contractions became so strong that they *had* to be labor pains. The big creature in the dark had horns and sharp teeth. The suitcase had long been packed and ready. Mari rolled it out to the yard and held Ida up. I packed my wheelchair full of all the small things we thought we would need, and together we waited for the taxi that would not have room for me.

The car bearing Ida and Mari vanished into the darkness. I followed behind in my wheelchair with my heart hammering. Through dim streets, empty streets, over the last bits of winter slush and gravel, the springtime had only dropped in for a short visit, I rode up past Alexander Kiellands plass, through the traffic lights in Uelands gate without waiting for them to turn green, continued along Kirkeveien. At night, it feels like the wheelchair moves quickly, much more quickly than the recorded miles per hour. And we arrived at the hospital at the same time, the taxi and my wheelchair.

Ida stood holding the nursing pillow, the one my sister had recommended, while Mari took the suitcase out of the taxi. It still didn't feel *real*, what was happening, it felt too much like what we had practiced. Because it so strongly resembled what we'd practiced, it therefore still had to be practice. It is a unique form of madness to believe that you can prepare for everything, to plan for all contingencies. To believe that you know what the unknown contains. It's a madness I cannot escape.

The windows and entrance of the clinic were dark, there was a strike on and normal operations were suspended. But we buzzed and were let in, we took the elevator up to the third floor and were given the birthing suite we had been hoping for, the suite we had agreed we should receive—if it was available. Every contract about bodies is signed with provisos.

We had hoped for this suite because the bed there was extra solid, large and high enough for me to lift myself up alone. This meant I could go get water for Ida if she needed it, I could be helpful while Mari sat kneeling up against Ida's back to help with the aches, help with the pain. We unpacked, pitched camp, rigged ourselves up.

Nothing happened, minutes ticked by.

We lay there and waited; the minutes turned to hours. At first, they came and attended to us, but after that they left us alone. Ida slept for a few hours, Mari and I watched and waited, the morning came. We went home, and it felt like a defeat.

Why did it feel like a defeat? We hadn't done anything wrong. We had gone when we thought we needed to go, we brought all the things we thought we might need. The room was available, it was meant for us. But we had been waiting for so long. All fall and winter we had been waiting.

We had been sitting in our living room for the last months, me on the sofa and Ida in the recliner that could be pushed flat, the recliner where she slept when she couldn't fall asleep anywhere else. We drank tea, read books, waited, waited, waited. A voice said (absurd): *Nothing will come of this. There won't be any child.*

But we had felt him kick, first only Ida, but then me too. He was coming. He was simply taking his time. A few weeks earlier he had been positioned crosswise, on the ultrasound it looked like he'd strung up a hammock in there, and we realized he might have to be born via C-section, that he didn't care about all our plans. But he turned, just as he had many times before, he had flipped around like an acrobat, and this time he put his head facing downward, right where it should be. We said to each other: *He's coming now.* And then we added: *Isn't he?*

Why do I write this?
What do I wish to tell?
How I became an adult.
How I became a human.
What changed.
What stayed the same.

I cannot rid myself of grief over the body that *was not.* Psychiatry keeps setting tighter limits on when grief stops being healthy and starts to become pathological, six months, three months, four weeks, grief becomes a sickness and sickness is something you are supposed to recover from. But grief is not like that, deep grief can last an entire lifetime, mine does. It's not the kind that tears me to pieces. It is a part of me. To live with it is to acknowledge that it exists and will continue to exist.

The grief is sometimes weak, sometimes strong. It was strong in the thought that my child would be able to master everything I will never master myself. There was grief in the thought that my child would have everything I never had. And then I discovered that it was precisely in the thought, in the expectation, that this grief dwelled. Whenever reality took over, it was a different story. The shadows dispersed.

My notion of my child is something other than my child. My notion of my child, before my child was born, was a memory of the child I was and of the child I could have been. But my child exists, here and now, he is the child who lives in the world.

This child who climbs and runs and hops: this child is not me. This child is himself. I saw this, and my grief moved, it shifted, it was no longer directed toward the future, but rather toward the past. Now the grief is, for me, about what didn't happen, for better or worse.

I missed so much when I was growing up: the experience of being physically free in any place other than the swimming pool, on dry land, together with all the other land animals running in a flock. I feel the grief over *this* rising up like a great wave. And then it swills slowly out again, every time.

Grief is a wave, but it is also aftermath, the stillness following a storm. This is its paradox. Grief lives just as well in the thought of what I escaped as it does in the thought of what I never had. Perhaps grief is simply the realization that time passes. It is the voice that says *never*, and it is also the voice that says *never again*.

When I read the old case notes, when I read the grim predictions, I know that I was saved, that my life is a story of survival. Then I think about everyone who is or was like me, those who were left behind.

Grief turns out to be a place none of us know until we reach it.

✣ ✣ ✣

One summer, toward the end of *life before Alexander*, Ida and I were in Copenhagen, in a greenhouse of the botanical garden. In one of the rooms, I recognized the scent of eucalyptus and saw that Ida noticed it too, the scent of eucalyptus here in Copenhagen, in a room of a greenhouse that simulated a climate very different from the Nordic climate. We had been in California together, the same memories were inside each of us. Ida was pregnant, she was only a few weeks along, we only suspected it at this point, we didn't know for sure yet. We were at the start of something new, and for a brief period it was okay that we didn't know anything for sure. The liminal space in the greenhouse in the botanical gardens: the sun and the pine needles and the scent of eucalyptus.

I am struck by a similar feeling each year in September, the clearest and most sun-drenched days, when the nights have turned chilly and the summer is over, then an echo of California reverberates through Oslo, which is where I now live, with my family.

I know a third grief as well, one that persists, that does not swill out again. It is grief over the world that does not exist, that will never exist, and this grief isn't melancholic, it is bitter and mingled with rage toward the world that exists in reality and does not have any space for me, that doesn't even want to make space for me.

I ask the question, *is this good enough?* and I know there will never be an answer.

I ask the question, *and what if I hadn't been able to achieve all of this?* and I know there will never be an answer.

I ask the question, *and what if things had gone the way the doctors expected it to, if I had lived the life that Social Services expected, if I had measured it out with*

*teaspoons instead of striking out toward a big, expansive
sky, what then, would my life have been less valuable,
and what about the others, those who didn't have a choice,
what about their lives?* and I know there is no answer I could possibly wish to hear.

I do not want to live a life of rage and grief. I write it off of me, I reject it.

*When the child was a child,
it had no opinions on things,
no habits,
sat mostly cross-legged,
leapt into a run,
a cowlick in its hair,
made no faces when photographed.*

Experience is not incontestable, but it is another form of knowledge than that which comes from reflection, it has a different substance. Experience turns words into something other than tokens, they become plants with deep roots and it hurts to pull them up.

My body is the same, but it has changed, marked by experiences. I have many scars, many wounds. My ankle will never be what it was, now it's my left foot that is the good one. Each winter weighs a little heavier than the last. The experiences settle themselves within me, the sediments sink to the bottom. I am no longer transparent, I am substance through and through.

I met you. We met.

I had begun to accept that the world was the way it was, but that was because I had begun to realize how much of it was not for me, for people such as me. I would like to believe that things will get better, though I fear that they won't. Some things don't get better, some things get worse. This is not a world that will ever embrace all of its people, this is not a world where there will ever be space for all. But it is not an unchangeable world, it gives in to pressure. There are cracks to be found in existence.

Doctor's note, September 21, 1988

Improvement of the condition should not be expected, it will most likely get worse, and it is therefore of utmost importance that circumstances are optimally arranged so as to allow him to lead as normal a life as possible with his family and in society. He has very good capabilities.

To put it in another way: *None of this is certain.*

I believe in the sublime, I believe in the force of the world as it is. I believe that the world is infinitely stronger than me, and yet I still attempt to bend it to my will. This cannot succeed through aimless exertion, only through deliberate hard work. It can only succeed if I look for the fractures, for the hairline glimmers of light coming through.

We said to each other: *If we are lucky, luckier than anyone is allowed to hope for, then one of us will, at some point in the future, be present when the other dies.*

✦ ✦ ✦

A few weeks before the due date, there was no space for anything other than the impending moment.

Our apartment was bigger than it had been. We had taken down a wall and annexed the rooms next door; when the dust settled and the furniture was moved back in, we had space for a family. We took out everything we owned and upended our home in expectation of the unknown.

Everything I have done has been *according to a plan*. I acted *as if*. When Ida came home with me, a double bed was there waiting, when she moved in, there was room for her things. Now our apartment had a nursery. This is also called *living in hope*.

Ida went a day over the due date, and then another, and then a week. During this week, we didn't live alone. We knew we would need help, and we were right about that, we just didn't know how much help we would need.

We had a plan, and that wasn't a bad thing. It was insufficient, but it wasn't bad. That night, we were certain that labor had begun. We went to the hospital, they let us stay until morning. Then we went back home, and Ida wondered if she had imagined the whole thing.

Two days later we were back, this time it was different. This time we would not be returning home alone.

During the first hours of the birth, we were in a large suite in the clinic where we had applied for a place. There was a double bed and a large bathtub, a platform walker so Ida could walk around with solid support, a rubber ball that she could sit on.

The double bed was the only thing we used. The amniotic fluid was discolored, and that's when everything changed, the clouds darkened. We were sent to the neighboring clinic, to a smaller room, full of medical equipment. Ida had a monitor hooked up to her and to the child that was still inside of her. The bed was a narrow hospital bed, and from the first, she felt the discomfort of confinement. This was in addition to the pains, which had long since begun to intensify.

There was no space for me. At first, I drove the wheelchair into the room, but that wouldn't do. A midwife came in, and then another, and I had to move. I went back and forth several times before realizing that the wheelchair would have to stay out in the corridor. After a while, we were able to have an extra bed wheeled in, over by the window. In the tiny pauses between contractions, I could rest there, while Mari could stretch out on the floor. Ida was inside a long, dark tunnel. At times she knew I was in the room, other times she didn't.

We were in the midst of uncertainty. None of us knew how long it would last, how bad it would be. This time was *kairos*, the moment filled the horizon. After a week of labor pains, after the false-alarm trip to the hospital two days earlier, Ida was exhausted. I was too. We tried to eat when we remembered to, tried to be sure Ida was taking in fluids and sugar.

By the time the surgeon made the decision to do a cesarean section, I had been expecting it for a long time. I was relieved, and scared to death. Ida hadn't understood that this was where we were headed. She fervently believed she could manage the birth herself, that it all came down to her willpower. It was never about willpower, or about strength. The fetal heartbeat was dropping because the umbilical cord was wrapped around our son's chest, and all of the willpower in the world could not loosen it. The body set the limits. Nonetheless, I loved Ida for that belief, for that hope.

I was not allowed to accompany them into the operating room. Even if I could put on the protective coveralls, there was no protective cover for my wheelchair. It was Mari who was allowed into the room, it was she who welcomed our son and was the first to hold him. We had known this might happen. We had asked Mari to come with us so that Ida wouldn't be alone no matter what. We had believed and we had hoped, and we had planned.

Ida and the doctors and Mari disappeared. I waited alone in the empty delivery room. It didn't take long, maybe three-quarters of an hour, but there was ample time to think. That moment, and those thoughts, I would prefer to forget.

And then Mari was there again, followed by a midwife with a little bundle in her arms. I lay down on the bed and received him and held him. He looked furious. With good reason, I thought. So, I held him. I held him until we were given permission to go in to see Ida. And then we were together, we three.

How quickly his body grew bigger, how quickly he grew strong and wild. I knew that he would one day be stronger than me. But for a long time, he slept on my chest, for a long time I carried him. His hair grew longer, but for a long time it was still only small wisps that curled in the wind from the sea, small wisps in the wind as he slept on me.

For a long time, I sat with a sleeping baby on my chest. Ida came into the room again. And then we were together, all three, on our way into the unknown.

Gratitude

This book has had many helpers and readers—direct and indirect, in earlier and later phases. Particular thanks to: Ida Jackson, Lars Grue, Fride Eeg-Henriksen, Kristin Grue, Vibeke Eeg-Henriksen, Arvid Heiberg, Sara Li Stensrud, Johanne Fronth-Nygren, Mari Wold Sannerud, Halvor Hanisch, Morten Moi, Harald Ofstad Fougner, Kari Marstein, and Espen Dahl.